Teaching the Trees

Teaching the Trees

Lessons from the Forest

JOAN MALOOF

THE UNIVERSITY OF GEORGIA PRESS

ATHENS AND LONDON

© 2005 by the University of Georgia Press
Athens, Georgia 30602
All rights reserved
Set in Aldus with Lorrenne display
Printed and bound by Thomson-Shore
Printed on 100% post-consumer processed chlorine-free paper.
The paper in this book meets the guidelines for permanence
and durability of the Committee on Production Guidelines
for Book Longevity of the Council on Library Resources.

PRINTED IN THE UNITED STATES OF AMERICA
09 08 07 06 05 c 5 4 3 2 1

LIBRARY OF CONGRESS CATALOGING-IN-PUBLICATION DATA
Maloof, Joan, 1956–
Teaching the trees : lessons from the forest / Joan Maloof.
        p. cm.
Includes bibliographical references.
ISBN 0-8203-2743-3 (hardcover : alk. paper)
1. Trees—East (U.S.)—Anecdotes. 2. Forest ecology—East (U.S.)—
Anecdotes. I. Title.
QK115.M155 2005
578.73'0974—dc22   2004030811
BRITISH LIBRARY CATALOGING-IN-PUBLICATION DATA AVAILABLE

FOR ALL HUMANS

WHO SPEAK UP TO DEFEND

THE LIVING THINGS

THAT HAVE NO VOICE

The Way In

Whoever you are: some evening take a step

out of your house, which you know so well.

Enormous space is near, your house lies where it begins,

whoever you are.

Your eyes find it hard to tear themselves

from the sloping threshold, but with your eyes

slowly, slowly, lift one black tree

up, so it stands against the sky: skinny, alone.

With that you have made the world. The world is immense

and like a word that is still growing in the silence.

In the same moment that your will grasps it,

your eyes, feeling its subtlety, will leave it. . . .

RAINER MARIA RILKE

TRANSLATED BY ROBERT BLY

CONTENTS

ILLUSTRATIONS

I am trusting that you love trees. It is not a difficult assumption; we all love trees. Even when we cannot name the species of the trees around us we still feel their magnificence, their power, their *presence*. We know that the world would be a less wonderful place if we no longer had towering trees to walk under, but we don't often think about what we would lose along with the trees.

A world of fascinating organisms depends on the trees for their survival. Some are familiar to us — such as the birds that flit across our yards — but others are more mysterious. What biologists understand about these forest-dwelling organisms is often difficult to learn because it is published only in specialized science journals.

When I walk through the forest I see a magical web of relationships. I want to share my perception of these webs with you. I want to preserve forests filled with old trees not only so you and I can walk in their presence, but to keep the whole web intact, alive. If you set out to learn about what goes on in a forest you will never be bored. The stories go on forever, and I have included just a few of them here.

Interwoven with the facts and the stories here is the poetry—mostly the poetry of Rainer Maria Rilke, which, like the forest, is a continuous source of new revelations to me. His "Ninth Elegy," which I quote from frequently, is printed in its entirety in the appendix.

This book is called *Teaching the Trees* because I teach many of these natural history stories in my biology courses at Salisbury University. But, of course, the trees are still teaching me too.

ABOUT THE ILLUSTRATIONS

The illustrations in this book were created over two hundred years ago. They are the work of artist-naturalist John Abbot. Abbot was very prolific, but only one published book gave him credit in the title; it is from that book that the illustrations are borrowed: *The natural history of the rarer lepidoterous insects of Georgia. Including their systematic characters, the particulars of their several metamorphoses, and the plants on which they feed. Collected from the observation of Mr. John Abbot, many years resident in that country* (London: printed by T. Bensley, for Sir James Edward Smith, 1797). The illustrations appear here courtesy of the Hargrett Rare Book and Manuscript Library, University of Georgia Libraries. The frontispiece appears courtesy of Special Collections, Hill Memorial Library, LSU Libraries, Baton Rouge, La.

It is obvious from Abbot's illustrations that he, too, was a lover of trees and had an interest in the organisms that lived among them. In this book, I discuss many tree species—and their animal partners—that Abbot never illustrated; conversely, Abbot painted many tree species and insects that I did not write about. The Abbot illustrations show some of the trees discussed in the text, but primarily they are here to stir the senses, to add another layer of wonder, and to show that I have barely begun to tell all there is to know of a forest. Readers wanting contemporary images of any of the tree species I write about may consult any common field guide to trees.

Teaching the Trees

Old-Growth Air

For years I have been explaining to the students in my classes that Maryland's Eastern Shore has no old-growth forests left, whatsoever; that this land the early explorers called Arcadia because of its numerous stately trees has been completely altered, and not a single original forest remains. Depending on my mood the day we discuss it, I relate this fact either with anger or with sadness. Last semester, however, I heard rumors that a twenty-acre remnant of old-growth forest remained. Twenty acres can barely be called a forest, but still I was anxious to see this unique scrap. So one spring morning when I awoke to a "true blue dream of a sky," I knew right away that this was the day I should visit the "leaping greenly spirit of trees."[1]

The forest was more than sixty miles away, and detailed directions were necessary to find it. Even before the car stopped on the isolated dirt road, a sweet, rich, earthy

smell filled my senses. I used to think that particular odor was the smell of the mountains, but here I was, still on flat land. Did my own ground once smell like that too—before the grandfather trees were gone, in a time when the trees' breath merged with that of the fungi and the birds and the insects?

When we discuss what we miss about forests after they have been cut, we usually mention the sight or the shade or the species; but now I was breathing deeply of a forest gift I had forgotten: the air! Americans largely ignore this dimension of the forest's allure, but the Japanese recognize it and have a name for it: *shinrin-yoku*—wood-air bathing. Japanese researchers have discovered that when diabetic patients walk through the forest, their blood sugar drops to healthier levels.[2] Entire symposiums have been held on the benefits of wood-air bathing and walking. I certainly feel better after a walk in the woods, but until I read about it, I didn't know there was a name for my therapy.

What could be in forest air that makes us feel better? Researchers working in the Sierra Nevada of California found 120 chemical compounds in the mountain forest air—but they could identify only 70 of them![3] We are literally breathing things we don't understand. And when we lose our forests, we don't know what we are losing. Some of the compounds in the air come from the bacteria and the fungi in the soil, but most are given off by the trees. Trees release volatile organic compounds from little pockets between their leaf cells. A number of theories exist about why they release the compounds. Possibly it is to deter insects. Or possibly the compounds are just metabolic by-products, and this is how trees eliminate them, having no excretory system. The scientific community is still undecided.

I like to think of these enticing fragrances as a sort of mutualistic reward for humans—a *Botany of Desire* scenario where the trees are using one of the few wiles they have that work on humans,[4] although in some cases, such as that of the sassafras tree, having a pleasing aroma is grounds for decimation. Native Americans used the sassafras medicinally, and European explorers were quick to adopt the fragrant leaves for both medicinal and culinary uses. The first shipment of sassafras was sent back to England in 1602, and sassafras remained the largest export for almost a hundred years.

It is not inconceivable that the trees may be altering our perceptions with their chemicals. The volatile molecules evaporate into the air and come into contact with the sensory neurons in our nasal passageways. The olfactory nerves send messages directly to the limbic system in our brains, which deals with instinctive emotions such as sex, memory, and aggression. The limbic system can certainly affect our physical bodies, and all of this can happen even without our perception of having "smelled" anything.

The molecules from the trees don't just go up our noses, however; they are also part of the air that goes into our lungs, and once in our lungs, some of the molecules can enter our bloodstreams. So when we walk through the forest inhaling that sweet air, the wood-air, the forest actually becomes a part of our bodies. No wonder that a forest walk evokes the lines from Rainer Maria Rilke's "Ninth Elegy":

> Earth, my dearest, I will. Oh believe me, no more
> of your springtimes are needed to win me over—, one,
> ah, a single one, is already too much for my blood.
> (72–74)[5]

Aromatherapy practitioners call these plant-produced volatile compounds "essential oils" and depend on handed-down folk wisdom to know the effects these various oils will have on the human body. Among the most abundant compounds given off by trees are monoterpenes. Aromatherapists claim that the monoterpenes in pine are antiviral and antiseptic, good for asthma and respiratory infections, but there is no medical research to back up their claim.

There has been a great deal of research, however, on *edible* monoterpenes, and these *have* been shown both to prevent and to cure cancer. Many chemotherapy drugs contain monoterpenes, but we can also find them in our own kitchens; lemon rinds, in particular, have large amounts of them. Could inhaling monoterpenes be a cancer cure as well? Is *shinrin-yoku* a valid therapy? And a bigger question: Why hasn't the Western medical community been researching the physical effects of inhaling the monoterpenes so abundant in forest air? Might it be because forest air cannot be patented, and consequently no money is to be made from it?

We decry the destruction of tropical rainforests, citing the wonder drugs that may eventually be found in them, but we may have miracle medicines lurking right beneath our own noses. Perhaps someday, when our physician asks us to "take a deep breath," it will be old-growth air that he or she is recommending.

I hope we don't have to drive too far to find it.

My discussion has wandered far from the old-growth forest I visited that clear blue day. It was a beautiful and magical place. I felt healthy and whole while I was there, and for hours afterward. Perhaps my walk even killed that cancer cell that was trying to establish itself in my breast. Others have said it before, but I'll say it again: Perhaps by trying to save the forests we are actually trying to save ourselves.

We know, instinctively, that our own health, both physical and spiritual, is a reflection of the health of the earth—for better or for worse. But we barely have words to discuss this connection, perhaps because we don't yet have all the tools needed to measure it. The strands connecting us are largely invisible. In the poem still running through my mind Rilke says:

> Earth, isn't this what you want: to arise
> in us invisible?—Earth! invisible! (68–69)

Most of us want to believe that something within us outlives our physical bodies. I think Rilke is exploring the idea that the things of this world want to tag along when we change form—and they can do that only if we take them into our hearts and build them into our invisible webs. "What if not transformation is your urgent commission?" he asks (71).

Many people are sensitive to these invisible connections; and those who are most conscious of the living web suffer the most when it is bombed, paved, or otherwise disrupted. Biologists are often attracted to the study of living things *because* we feel these connections. Learning the details about the interactions of the myriad living things on the earth only deepens our concern for them. Biologists frequently become champions and protectors for the organisms they study: To know them is to love them. And so biologists, like poets, have a special role to play in helping us stay aware of the connections—and a special obligation to speak out when the web of life is abused and disrupted.

Breathe deeply; we are about to take a walk through the trees.

Tulip Poplar

My first experience with tulip poplar trees (*Liriodendron tulipifera*) made a lasting impression on me, but I had no idea
then that it was the beginning of a long relationship. Back
in the days when fourth-graders could hang out without
parental supervision, my best buddy and I were practicing
to be circus performers, specifically tightrope walkers. Our
tightrope was a metal cable hung between wooden posts.
The cable was not there to foster juvenile circus fantasies; it
had been installed by the highway department to keep cars
from spilling down the steep, wooded hillside. While await-
ing my turn on the high wire, I looked down at the ground
and saw a tuliplike flower with green and orange petals. I
had no idea where this beautiful flower had come from until
I looked up into the trees overhead and noticed other flowers
like it there. Tulips that grew on trees! How magical!

I sometimes ask others about their childhood memories

of plants. It turns out that many people have a very specific memory of a particular plant species, a memory of wonder, awareness, connection—sometimes almost to the point of fear. If you carry such a memory, you have probably tried to learn (though perhaps years later) the name of the plant that held you spellbound. I learned that my beautiful flower came from a tulip poplar tree. Some books call it a yellow poplar, but it will always be a tulip poplar to me.

AS FATE WOULD HAVE IT, I renewed my acquaintance with that species years later when I was an undergraduate studying the fungal diseases of plants. My faculty adviser was interested in a fungal disease of tulip poplar trees, and I found myself doing a scientific research project, my first, on *Liriodendron tulipifera*. I learned that a fungus named *Verticillium* can enter the tree roots and cause a disease that eventually kills the tree, either by physically blocking the water passageways or by producing a toxin. Our research project was designed to discover which of these two mechanisms was responsible for the tree's death.

After months of work in the laboratory I determined that the wilt was caused by a toxin. The procedure to purify the toxin involved a lot of glassware and drop-by-drop precision. By the time I got the toxin purified it was time to graduate, so I wrote up my senior thesis: "Isolation of a Lipoprotein from Culture Filtrates of *Verticillium albo-atrum*." It was my first taste of real science, and among other things it taught me that I was better suited to field biology than laboratory research.

Be careful what you wish for. My most recent experience with a tulip poplar tree was sleeping in the top of one! You have probably heard of tree sitters: people who live for a time in the treetops to prevent a forest from being cut.

The tactic has been used a number of times, and sometimes it is successful. But how do you practice to be a tree sitter? How do you learn the techniques and decide if tree sitting is really for you? The best-known tree sitter of them all, Julia Butterfly Hill, began without any practice whatsoever. The first time she climbed up a redwood tree she was participating in a protest; the second time up she stayed for two years—protecting the tree's life with her own.[1] For the more cautious among us there is the Eastern Forest Defense Action Camp.

Summer camp for radicals seemed the perfect antidote to the heart-crunching pain I felt driving by yet another clear-cut forest every week. At the camp a guerrilla activist half my age taught me how to climb trees using ropes and a harness. She and her friends had rigged a piece of board, about the size of a door, sixty feet up in a tall tulip poplar tree. After I proved myself capable of the climb she asked if I wanted to try spending the night up there. Yes, please. When I climbed up to the small platform in the dark, hauling my water bottle and sleeping bag up behind me, I wasn't expecting to get much sleep. I had to wear my harness at all times, complete with carabiners and ropes, and clip in to a rope tied around the tree to make sure I didn't roll off the platform and fall to my death. Sleeping in a tree gives a whole new dimension to falling out of bed. As uncomfortable as it sounds, I was happy to be "clipped in," and to my astonishment I fell right to sleep. I woke once in the night and got to experience the sounds of the nocturnal canopy—the flying squirrels moving from branch to branch and chirping to each other. It was much more blissful than frightening, and when I woke at dawn I was happy to see that I was still up in the tree. Up where the flowers are.

TULIP POPLARS have big, showy flowers—the ones that amazed me in my childhood—to attract pollinators. The flowers have to be pollinated within twenty-four hours after opening or no seeds will form. Insects carry the pollen from one flower to another. If there are no other tulip poplar trees nearby, the insects can self-pollinate the flowers, but self-pollinated flowers do not produce as many seeds, and the resulting seedlings are not as vigorous.

The abundant nectar produced by the flowers rewards the pollinating bees, and also the humans lucky enough to find the tulip poplar honey made by the bees. The trees must grow for almost twenty years before they reach "puberty" and begin flowering, but once they do they can produce flowers for another two hundred years. Each flower produces only about ten good seeds. The seeds, winged at one end, flutter to the forest floor in the fall and stay, alive but dormant, waiting up to seven years for an opportunity to sprout—that is, if the birds and squirrels don't eat them first. Cardinals, in particular, are fond of tulip poplar seeds, and they gather beneath the trees, sifting the soil with their beaks as they look for the tasty morsels.

Tulip poplar seedlings are easy to start. All you have to do is go to a forest where tulip poplars grow, scoop up some soil from the forest floor, spread it in a shallow tray, and put the tray in a spot where it will get some light and you will remember to keep it moist. The seedlings are a favorite nibble for rabbits and deer, so be sure to put your seedlings in a place where animals cannot get to them. Food for bees, humans, cardinals, squirrels, rabbits, and deer—to name just a few—these trees are more than just wood.

These are the connections that interest me now: from sun to leaf cell to nectar to seed to bee to bird to me, an ecologist. The word *ecologist* comes from the Greek word for "house." And I am striving to learn all that I can about this house, this home, of mine. It is a humbling task. There is much to learn. Charles Bowden, another forest ecologist, described the feeling in his book *The Secret Forest*:

> I sensed I had wandered into that house we call ecology, a place that pretends to be carefully mapped but always turns out to be a labyrinth. The structure may have an edge but it seems to have no center. The forest is a question that we will never answer.[2]

Come wander through the forest labyrinth with me, and we will take a lesson from another ecologist that Bowden wrote about:

> But Gentry was too alert and too alive to keep a single focus and things besides the taxonomy of the forest continually spill into his writings. He never let his love of plants blind him to his love of life. Nor should anyone else who wishes truly to savor the elements that lurk in that single English word, *place*.[3]

Tree Hugger

My students are not used to hearing someone speak with such tenderness, with such fiercely protective words, about the nonhuman things of this world. It makes them a bit uncomfortable; they wiggle in their seats. I know that each of them really longs to find something to care about deeply. But they are still wondering, waiting for the thing that will claim them, like this living world has so obviously claimed me, their teacher. I cannot teach them their place, define their passion. I can only assure them that they do have one.

In some aboriginal cultures the entire community helps young people find their unique place in the world. Skills are explored, dreams are discussed, and the whole village leads each young person to the path of his or her life's journey. This attitude makes wonderful sense to me, but unfortunately our young people get no such help today. I do not have the time or the energy to guide each of the one

hundred students I have every semester for fourteen weeks, just a few days a week, a few hours a day.

Their parents want me to help their children find something they can be passionate about, and I do what I can. But I feel about as helpful as a cartographer wearing a straightjacket trying to draw a map with a pen held between his teeth. My efforts to help them are crude. And while they wait to be claimed by a passion, many try to fill the emptiness with sports scores or hip-hop music or alcohol. The best I can do is to show them that what they are seeking is possible to find, and that longing for it is nothing to be ashamed of.

The most courageous thing a teacher of teenagers and young adults can do is to try to break through the cool demeanor our usual interactions require. Bare the depths of your feelings; show what moves you. In doing so you will expose yourself to ridicule; that is why it takes courage. You must be brave enough to bear the laughter.

The best teachers know this already, and it is not just in my classroom that students see a different, deeper, way of being in the world. Their literature teacher is moved by the poems of a certain poet, and they can feel some warmth from that fire themselves. They respect the admiration their philosophy teacher feels for a particularly brilliant mind; they sense the indescribable flood of emotion created in their painting teacher by a particular piece of art, or in their math teacher by an elegant theorem. They are familiar with humans celebrating the creations of other humans — a beautiful and good thing — but they are less accustomed, I sense, to seeing a human celebrating the nonhuman. Wonder? awe? respect? for a *paramecium*? a *snail*? a *tree*? I try to show them that these things, too, are worthy of praise, of rescue.

Rilke says:

> —And these things,
> that live by going away, know that you praise them; fleeting,
> they look to us for rescue, us, the most fleeting of all.
> They want us to transform them completely in our invisible
>> heart
> into—oh infinitely—into ourselves. Whoever finally we
>> will be. (63–67)

Emotion and poetry in a biology class make the students squirm. They whisper to each other: "Dr. Maloof is a tree hugger." And they laugh when I tell them that, yes, I have hugged trees. When I tell them that I'm going to make them hug trees, too, I hear more nervous laughter. They seem almost afraid of the prospect, like I'm going to make them skydive, although I suspect that most of them would rather jump out of a plane than hug a tree.

When we go to the forest on our field trip I am true to my word and I do have them hug a tree. Not because I find tree hugging to be an ecstatic experience; in fact, to me, hugging trees feels silly. I have heard of people who had an epiphany while hugging a tree, but I'm not one of them. If you've never tried it, I encourage you to find out for yourself. So why make them do it? I think it is because "tree hugger" is a label. They have labeled me, just like the vitriolic radio talk show host, the CEO of the office supply store, and the chief of the U.S. Forest Service have labeled me. Now, because they have hugged a tree, they share the label. And they can see that the label means nothing. They are no different because they have hugged a tree. And yet these students—non–science majors who are taking a biology class because they "have to"—can no longer point derisory fingers at the "crazy tree huggers." They will never again be able to use that term dismissively, because they too have hugged a tree.

You are now in on my secret. You know some of the other things I try to teach (passion, compassion) at the same time I am covering the official course curriculum (the classification of living organisms, the steps of photosynthesis, the workings of DNA). I take a risk when I admit that I am trying to teach more than just biology, but I am not alone. Other teachers have taken the risk before me. Parker Palmer, in his book *The Courage to Teach*, wrote: "As I teach, I project the condition of my soul onto my students, my subject, and our way of being together."[1] Yes, Parker. Whoever, finally, we will be, let us pray it is worthy of being passed along.

Sycamore

I have been intimate with sycamore trees: my nose an inch from the bark, my arms wrapped around the trunk, my skinny schoolgirl legs stretching for the next branch. I am a climber of sycamore trees (*Platanus occidentalis*). The trees and I grew up together in the same suburban neighborhood. Standing atop a chain-link fence surrounding one of the half-acre lots was a good way to reach the first branch. After that it was all flexibility and daring until I dared to go no further and found a spot to rest . . . and look down.

As I get older I rehearse the concept of my own mortality more frequently, but being far up in that tree was my first opportunity to practice.

"I will die."

"I could die at any moment."

"One wrong move and I could die right now."

In many ways it was a thrilling and freeing thought.

I don't know if the attitude, the altitude, or the solitude had the greatest effect on me in that tree, but up there I had a completely different perspective on the rest of the world. There I could be myself, a distinct individual not shaped by parents or teachers or friends, but shaped instead by some mysterious universal force to fulfill some unknown void in the web. High up in that sycamore tree I had my first taste of self-actualization. It makes me wonder if my life would have turned out differently had I no big trees to climb.

Years later, I was interested to read that another climber of sycamore trees is mentioned in the Bible. Luke 19 tells the story of Zaccheus, who climbed a sycamore tree because he was trying to "see who Jesus was." It was the only way he could see over the throngs of people who had gathered to see Jesus as he passed through Jericho. When Jesus passed under the tree he looked up and saw Zaccheus there.

"Hurry and come down," Jesus said, "for today I must stay at your house."

Although the species of sycamore in America is not the same one that grew in Jericho, I still like the story — I like the idea that Jesus had a fondness for tree climbers.

AS A SYCAMORE TREE GROWS, the outer layer of bark cannot keep up and eventually peels off in flakes. This is happening in my yard as I write, in the midst of the dog days of summer. Underneath the peeling flakes the branches are smooth and white. The result is a pattern of tan, olive, and white patches, making the tree look as if its skin were peeling from its bones. During the summer months the leaves hide the nakedness of the white bark; but after the leaves have fallen, in the bright light of a winter afternoon, the sycamore tree resembles a huge skeleton standing guard over the landscape.

SYCAMORE TREES are the most massive trees in the eastern United States. They can grow over a hundred feet tall and as much as ten feet wide. They can live for up to five hundred years. When they get very old, sycamores tend to form a cavity at the ground level. These cavities eventually get large enough for a child to enter and play "fort." Perhaps you remember playing in such a tree yourself?

Rural legends claim that the early settlers used these huge old hollowed-out trees as shelters for their livestock, keeping them out of the weather and protected from predators—a sort of poor man's barn. Besides being places for children's play and farm animals, sycamore trees have also been called home by grown men and women. The most famous of the sycamore homes was the one occupied by brothers Sam and John Pringle. The young, destitute brothers enlisted in the British army in the late 1750s, primarily to get free passage to America, and were stationed at a fort in what is now West Virginia. Eventually Sam and John decided to desert and headed off into the wilds to avoid capture. In the forest they met a solitary trapper. The brothers spent a few years with him, trapping and living off the bounty of the land. They had no money, but they managed to stay alive and free. Eventually the Pringle brothers had an argument with the trapper and went out on their own. It was then that they found the hollow sycamore tree that gave them protection: from the weather, the local Indians, and the British soldiers who were searching for them. They lived in the tree for three years.

When they learned that the war was over and they no longer had to fear capture, the brothers traveled back to civilization with stories of the wonderful fertile valley where they had been living in a tree. They convinced a small band of pioneers to establish a settlement with them in the val-

ley. During that time Sam met and married young Charity Cutright, who lived with him inside the tree after John graciously moved out.[1] I wish I could speak with Charity and learn what she thought of living inside a sycamore tree! Perhaps someday I will spend the night in one myself.

HUMANS AND LIVESTOCK are not the only creatures who consider sycamore trees a suitable dwelling place. In 1993 a group of biologists discovered a colony of rare bats living inside a hollow sycamore. While mist-netting bats they captured a rare Indiana bat (*Myotis sodalis*). They attached a radio transmitter to the bat and released it. When they searched for it the next day using a radio receiver, they discovered that the bat was roosting in a sycamore tree about a mile and a half from where they had captured it. The roost was a maternity colony, containing lactating females and their young. The researchers could count the bats and determine how many were using the tree by stationing themselves outside the tree at sunset when the bats headed out to feed. It turned out that there were almost a hundred bats living in that sycamore tree.[2]

THE INTERIOR OF THE TRUNK isn't the only place where creatures live. If you look closely at a sycamore leaf you will notice that it is not evenly green. There are pale yellowish areas on the leaf where the green seems to have been scraped off. These lighter areas are caused by insects feeding on the cells on the underside of the leaf. The insects scrape or suck everything out of the cell, including the green-pigmented chloroplasts, creating the pale mottling you see on the upper side of the leaf.

Sycamore trees have many insect partners that are found on no other plants. One of the most beautiful of these is the tiny sycamore lace bug (*Corythuca ciliata*). Imagine armor made of hardened lace with clear panels between the lace strands, and you get an idea of the fascinating appearance of these little bugs. They are visible to the naked eye, but a magnifying glass is necessary to really appreciate their beauty. Chances are you will find them on most of the sycamore leaves you examine. No sycamore trees: no sycamore lace bugs.

The sycamore leafhopper (genus *Erythroneura*) is another insect that feeds only on sycamore leaves. There are six species of these leafhoppers, and the only way to tell them apart is to examine the male's genitalia under a powerful microscope. The females can't be told apart at all. As a scientist I understand the impulse toward minutiae that so often confounds others, but even I have a hard time imagining who took the time to examine the genitalia of insects no bigger than a grain of rice.

Mark McClure, a researcher in Illinois, spent a year studying five species of tiny insects he found on the underside of sycamore leaves.[3] He learned that the different species feed on different parts of the leaves. For instance, some species were never found feeding on the veins, and others were almost always found feeding on the veins. The insects were doing what biologists call "partitioning the resource" — sharing. Of the five species that McClure studied, only one, the potato leafhopper (*Empoasca fabae*), did not feed and breed exclusively on sycamore. The other four insect species ate, copulated, and laid eggs on the sycamore leaves. When the leaves dropped from the trees in the fall, the insects rode them down to the ground and found a place in the leaf litter to survive the winter. These little insects lived through snow and ice and in the spring flew back up to the newly emerging sycamore leaves.

The potato leafhopper (the nonexclusive insect), however, cannot survive freezing temperatures. When fall arrives it must migrate to the south. You have doubtless heard of the migration of monarch butterflies, whose long journey seems miraculous enough, but we are talking here about an insect that looks like a green sesame seed with wings—a thing so small that it cannot fly against the wind. The leafhopper depends on the wind patterns to carry it to warmer temperatures where it can survive; and so this tiny thing joins the ranks of the aeroplankton: living things in the air.

How do the leafhoppers know how to catch the winds headed south in the fall and north in the spring? Scientists who have studied that question believe that just the right combination of light wavelength, pressure change, and temperature induces the leafhoppers to begin flying.[4] Once in flight they are carried into the air mass that rides high over a front and are, if luck is with them, taken in the direction they need to go.[5] The tiny insects can travel six hundred miles this way—an amazing feat. I certainly hope they don't end up on my windshield.

I KNOW of nine insect species that depend entirely on sycamore trees, and there may be more. So if we remove all the sycamore trees we will not only disrupt the development of young human girls and boys, but nine other species may be lost as well. When I explained this to a visiting friend he said, "So it's not like the trees are in the environment; it's like the trees *are* the environment." Yes, my friend, you get it.

Beech

I have fallen in love with beech trees (*Fagus grandifolia*). I was always fond of them, but over the years my affection has ripened into something deeper—something I'm not afraid to use the "L word" to describe.

The light inside a beech forest changes with each season, but always there is a radiance that makes your heart beat faster. The leaves are more translucent than the leaves of other types of trees, so more light passes through them; and the light takes on the hue of the leaves: pale green in the spring, lime green in the summer, and clear yellow in the fall. Even in the winter the trees are decorated for the season, with a few parchment-colored leaves hanging on, and perhaps some pine needle tinsel caught on the horizontal branches. The lower branches tend to droop down, sometimes forming a magical sanctuary full of that unreal light. Tell me, how can you not be in love with beech trees?

I USED TO WORK for the state of Maryland looking for rare and endangered plants. My botanist friend and I tramped through every kind of forest and habitat on Maryland's Eastern Shore. The days we got to spend time in a beech forest were special. People here take them for granted, but the reality is that only 2 percent of the forests in our area are beech forests, and all of them are on private land. That means that not one of them is protected from logging, and the rest of us have no say at all about what happens to them. If the landowners cut down every single beech forest in the state, it would be perfectly legal and acceptable in the eyes of the government. It makes me wonder about the wisdom of depending on the government to protect the environment.

One of my favorite beech forests, full of big, old trees, was in an area called Nutter's Neck. We visited the forest early one spring and had fun finding red-backed salamanders (*Plethodon cinereus cinereus*) hiding under branches on the damp forest floor. I had never seen so many salamanders in my life! Although a herpetologist will tell you that redbacks are the most common salamanders in the northeastern United States, it is still a thrill to find them. These little amphibians have no lungs, so they have to get their oxygen by absorbing it through their skin. The absorption mechanism works only if the skin is damp, so dry equals death to the salamanders. As you might imagine, a good rain brings them out in droves. They scamper around on the ground licking up ants, beetles, spiders, snails, and grubs. At night they climb trees looking for food. The salamanders literally stuff themselves when conditions are favorable, and live off their stored fat when conditions are too dry to forage.[1]

The salamanders typically live in forests that contain older deciduous trees, such as the one we were working in. They don't do well in pure pine forests because the needles that drop to the ground under the pines are very acidic and the acidity interferes with the salamander's "skin breathing."

ODORS ARE A VITAL PART of the red-backed salamander's world. An individual can smell another salamander and tell if it is a relative or not, and can tell by an area's odor whether it is in some other salamander's territory. Scent is also important for mating. The male will rub his scent on a female to stimulate her to breed. When both partners are ready, the male will deposit onto the forest floor a small, egg-shaped object that contains sperm. The female follows behind him and picks up the "sperm egg" with her cloaca (the amphibian equivalent of a vagina).[2] Those ignorant of salamander lifestyles might imagine that the salamander mothers just deposit their eggs in a suitable spot and then forget about them. Nothing could be further from the truth. After she lays her fertilized eggs down in a dark crevice of the earth, the female salamander will literally protect them with her life. She stays curled around the eggs—not even venturing out to feed—until they hatch. Salamander eggs that are not in contact with the female become infested with fungus and die. Scientists recently discovered that the female salamander's skin is inhabited by bacteria that prevent the growth of the egg-attacking fungus.[3]

AMONG THE INTERESTING PLANTS we often found growing under beech trees during our surveys was the appropriately named beech-drops (*Epifagus virginiana*). The plants may grow more than a foot tall, but it is easy to miss them because they have no green leaves at all—they are a purplish-brown color that blends in with the browns of the forest floor. They lack green leaves because they do not photosynthesize. Most plants have to photosynthesize to make sugars, the source of their energy, but beech-drops live off the sugars produced by the beech tree. The roots of the beech-drops tap into the roots of beech trees and pilfer the sugars needed for growth and reproduction. There is no evidence that the beech-drops harm the trees; it takes very little energy, after all, to support a small plant on the forest floor.

The beech-drops' flowers are so small that you need a magnifying lens to see them well. They reproduce by seed, like most plants, but unless the seed falls near a beech tree, the seedling is doomed. No beech tree: no beech-drops. There's always a price for letting someone else do all the work.

Beech-drops have a special place in my heart because they evoke a cherished memory. Long ago when I was an undergraduate studying plant science, some married friends of mine bought their first home. The house was in the suburbs, but their lot was full of trees, including beech trees. The lawn was too shady to support lawn grasses, so the soil was covered by moss. The first year my friends were in their new home, mysterious brown things poked up from beneath the moss. Were they fungi? Were they plants? Because I was a plant science major I was charged with finding out. I brought the things in to show to my botany professor, but he was young and new in his job and he didn't know what they were either. He asked me to leave them with him. Later in the day I looked in and saw him surrounded by open books while he examined the mystery plants under a microscope. The next day he told me that they were called beech-drops and shared the information I have already told you here. I reported back to the new homeowners, who were pleased with their plants, which were unusual in the suburbs and not for sale in any catalog or nursery. I think back fondly on those days because now I am the one with the books and the microscopes, uncovering the mysteries of nature for others.

IN THE BEECH FOREST that day, my botanist friend and I also found another plant that you can easily walk by without noticing: the tway-blade orchid (*Listera australis*). This tiny plant has only two leaves, each just a bit bigger than a thumbnail, and somehow manages to survive in the deep shade under beech trees. The plant we found was blooming, but these flowers, also, were so small that we needed a magnifying lens to examine them. Why were we excited by this tiny little thing? Because it was an orchid! All field botanists get excited when they find wild orchids, perhaps because they understand better than others the long and perilous path orchids must follow to reach maturity.

Orchids are notorious for having complex relationships with their pollinators. The minuscule flowers we were looking at were so inconspicuous that a bee would never bother visiting them. The western species of the tway-blade orchid, and probably the eastern species, too, depends on fungus gnats to carry its pollen from plant to plant.[4] The fungus gnat looks like a mosquito minus the sharp proboscis. After the gnats mate, the female lays her eggs on the damp forest floor where there is organic matter, such as old leaves, being consumed by fungi. The eggs hatch into larvae that resemble something you would wash from the corner of your eye, and the larvae begin feeding on the fungi—either on the threadlike mycelia or on the fungus fruits we call mushrooms. In time the larvae pupate and emerge as adult gnats. If the orchid is fortunate, it is blooming at the same time that the adult gnats are emerging. When one of the tiny flowers gets pollinated it begins to form seeds.

The seeds of most plants contain starchy food to nourish the embryonic plants as they germinate and grow toward the sunlight. Humans (and other animals) often eat seeds such as corn, beans, and wheat, usurping this starchy nourishment for ourselves. The bigger the seed, the more food is stored inside. Orchid seeds, however, are microscopic, dustlike particles. They contain a tiny embryo, but no food for it. The orchid seed cannot germinate and grow until it comes in contact with the right type of fungus. If the "right" fungus breaks through the wall of the orchid seed, the tiny embryo will begin to grow—feeding off the moisture and nutrients in the fungus. No gnats, no fungus: no orchids.

There are probably connections we don't yet understand between the fungus that enables the orchid seeds to germinate, the fungus that lives on fallen beech leaves, and the fungus that feeds the gnat larvae.

AND SO IT IS that beech trees provide habitat for many species: the red-backed salamanders, beech-drops, twayblade orchids, fungus gnats, and many fungal species. This is just the beginning of the list. I have not even mentioned the seeds of the beech and the organisms the seeds support.

A beech tree normally does not start producing seeds until it is forty years old. Unlike the orchid, the beech tree *does* store food in the seeds containing its plant embryos. The triangular beechnuts are encased in a prickly husk, two or three nuts to a case. In the fall the husk splits open and the nuts fall to the ground. The nuts can be eaten by many creatures, including humans—hence the Latin name for the beech tree genus, *Fagus*, which is Greek for "to eat." I have nibbled on beechnuts, but I'm not patient enough to collect the amount necessary for a meal. If I were like the native peoples, and had no grocery store nearby, I might reconsider.

In addition to the squirrels, mice, birds, and other small creatures that depend on the beechnuts for food, the nuts are a critical food source for bears. The movement patterns and territory of a bear will include beech forests if there are any nearby. For the bear, beechnuts can mean the difference between survival and starvation. Sadly, there are no bears in "my" beech forests. The last one in this area was killed around 1900.

FIRST WE KILL the bears, then we kill the beech forests. When my botanist friend and I visited the forest again, most of it had been cut down. We were there on a Sunday, so the loggers were not working, but the silence made the sight even sadder. The freshly cut stumps were wet with sap, and the surrounding trees were waiting for their turn to die. The felled trees were not going to be used to build homes or furniture. They were going to be pushed into a pile to rot or be burned; at most they would go to the chip mill and be turned into pulp for making cardboard. The owner of the forest would get very little money for the trees. Why, then, was he (or she) having them cut? The beech trees were being removed because they weren't valuable (in current economic terms), and because forty years from now they would just be a little bigger and still not valuable. But if the old beech trees were cut down and pines were planted in their place, in forty years the landowner could get a good price for the pine timber. And when that pine timber was cut, the land could be planted with pine again. Most likely we were witnessing the last beech forest ever to stand on that piece of ground. Good-bye red-backed salamanders who cannot live in the acid pine forests, good-bye beech-drops that cannot feed on pine roots, and good-bye tway-blade orchids that cannot survive the heavy equipment and herbicide sprays that are part of logging here. We have already said good-bye to the bears.

THE STATE OF MARYLAND, and probably your state, too, hires foresters with tax dollars. One semester I took my ecology students out to see the local "demonstration forest" run by the state forestry department. The purpose of the forest was to show landowners different forestry methods, but all I could see were pine trees, most of them very young. I asked if there was a natural forest that we could see for comparison. "No, sorry," was the answer. "There is a little corner of the property, I think, but it's too hard to get to, too muddy." I guess natural forests were not supposed to be demonstrated. The forester did teach my students how to estimate the dollar value of the trees where we were standing, but that was not exactly the lesson I had in mind for an ecology class. I asked him if private landowners ever requested forestry advice from him. He said, yes, it was an important part of his job. I asked what he would advise someone who owned a forest full of big old beech trees. He said that if they wanted an economic return on their land, he would advise them to clear-cut the beech trees and plant pine.

I wiped the dust from my feet as I left that place.

"God doesn't like a clearcut," Janisse Ray explains in her book *Ecology of a Cracker Childhood*.[5]

You'd better be pretty sure that the cut is absolutely necessary and be at peace with it, so you can explain it to God, for it's fairly certain he's going to question your motives, want to know if your children are hungry and your oldest boy needs asthma medicine—whether you deserve forgiveness or if you're being greedy and heartless. . . . Pine plantations dishearten God.

How many people, following a forester's advice, have cut a native forest to get more money to put in the bank or to buy a vacation home or to "get even" because they paid taxes on the property all these years or just to "leave something for the kids"?

I know men who think that a shrewd business deal—one they can make money on quickly—is a sign of their intelligence. They'll buy beautiful wooded land, sell the timber, plant pines, then sell the degraded property ("improved" in the eyes of the bank) and reap a large profit. These men think that they are smarter than I am because they have more money in the bank than I do. I feel sorry for them in a way; but mostly I feel sorry for the generation born after them.

PERHAPS THE ONLY WAY to ensure that future generations will get to see a beech forest is to buy one of the few left and protect it yourself. Two of my good friends did just that. When they were looking for land to build a house on they found a twenty-four-acre beech forest for sale. The owners were planning to cut the trees to sell as pulp and then sell the land. In addition to the sale price of the land, my friends paid the owners the amount they would have made on the pulp, and thereby were able to save the trees.

Their little forest was full of beautiful beech, chestnut oak, maple, and sweet gum trees, and during the house construction they tried to save as many of them as possible. They marked the trees to be saved, roped them off, and gave the contractors very specific instructions not to damage the trees. When the house was finally finished and the landscaping was completed, one by one the "protected" beech trees near the construction site died. Beech trees have shallow, sensitive roots, and the heavy trucks driving over the roots killed the trees even though the trunks were not touched. Beech trees are also very sensitive to minor changes in grade caused by construction; they need undisturbed soil to reach their full potential.

THINKING OF MY FRIENDS' BEECH FOREST brings to mind another special inhabitant of the older deciduous forests. My friends' new house had a big window looking out over the yard. In front of the window stood one of those dead beech trees with a dish full of birdseed at its base. By day the feeder was popular with many types of birds, but the real enchantment came at night. In the light of the outdoor spotlight shining on the feeder, we could see quick little southern flying squirrels (*Glaucomys volans*) zooming down to snatch a few seeds and then zipping off again. I was thrilled to see them. Flying squirrels inhabit many of Maryland's older forests, and I had learned to recognize the high-pitched noises they make at night, but hearing them and seeing them are very different things. Scientists don't usually use such terms, but I'll come right out and say it: southern flying squirrels are just too cute—small, not much bigger than your hand, with big, round eyes. They are completely nocturnal and forage through the forest in the dark. Nuts, such as beechnuts and acorns, are favored food items, and that at least partly explains the absence of these animals from young pine plantations. Unlike other squirrels, which crack nuts open, flying squirrels use their sharp teeth to cut a dainty hole in the shell. Take a look at the acorns on the ground next time you're in a forest to see if flying squirrels live there.

FLYING SQUIRRELS' RESTRICTED NESTING requirements are another reason they do better in older forests. Cavities in dead trees, spots where large old branches have broken off or where woodpeckers have made nesting holes, are the favored nests of the flying squirrels, and these are more abundant in older forests. Secure nests far from the ground and predators are especially important for females. Newborn flying squirrels weigh less than a chocolate-covered cherry. These tiny, hairless creatures cannot hear or see. Their skin is so translucent that their internal organs are visible through it. Obviously, such delicate creatures need weeks of care from a devoted mother.

Flying squirrels are surprisingly unterritorial about their nests. Especially in cold weather, the philosophy seems to be "the more the merrier." Large groups congregate in these winter nests and huddle together for warmth.

When my friends were having the dead beech tree in their yard removed, a group of squirrels jumped from a hole in the tree as it was on its way down. I have heard other stories of someone cutting a dead tree only to learn, too late, that it was a nesting space. Such stories should remind us of the important role that even seemingly useless dead trees play in the ecosystem.

Older forests that contain some dead and decaying wood also support abundant fungi, another favorite food of flying squirrels. Fungal spores pass through a squirrel's digestive system unharmed, so the squirrels may be helpful in spreading the fungi to new areas of the forest. Researchers found that northern flying squirrels (*Glaucomys sabrinus*) can spread spores from a mycorrhizal fungus that forms a symbiotic relationship with tree roots.[6] Trees that have this fungal partner are more successful. So squirrel helps fungus, fungus helps tree, and tree helps squirrel.

IT IS A PARADOX we must live with: even when we try to do the right thing we sometimes destroy habitat. But all animals do that when making their homes—living on the earth requires harming other organisms. I have come to believe that the only moral solution to the paradox is to strive to minimize our impacts and to be utterly clear about the impacts we are having. By opening our hearts to our victims—instead of trying to ignore them—we become more sensitive, more whole. And perhaps doing this may teach us more about how to live within the complexities of life's web. Maybe even the sorrow we feel for the organisms we destroy is part of the invisible web of life. I turn to Rilke again, a different poem this time, "What Survives":

Who says that all must vanish?
Who knows, perhaps the flight
of the bird you wound remains,
and perhaps flowers survive
caresses in us, in their ground.[7]

My friends plan to protect the twenty remaining acres of their beech forest. We hope the squirrels survived, that they found another suitable nest elsewhere in the forest. They have certainly survived in our hearts.

Pine

The long-needled loblolly pine (*Pinus taeda*) is responsible for the texture of the landscape around me. I live on a forested peninsula, and it is forested because loblolly pine trees sell for good money. So we grow pines here—but not for too long. We don't let them grow long enough to mature and slow in their growth; before that happens we cut them down and start over again, with new pines. Tree species other than pines are cut down to make room to plant more pines. That is a gross generalization, of course; but this is most likely what will happen to any piece of land that is not farmland or a building site.

The market drives the landscape. We live on a paper plantation. The forests here are composed mostly of loblolly pines because pines are useful for making paper and because they are among the few tree species that can be planted and harvested twice in a human's lifetime.

You might think I would be tired of loblolly pines, with so many of them growing all around me, but actually I feel love and compassion for them. To me, looking at a plantation of young pines is like looking at a nursery school classroom full of delightful children and knowing that none of them will live long enough to get gray hair or be a grandparent. I once hosted a Deep Ecology workshop that included a ceremony called the Council of All Beings. Following instructions from the workshop leader, we all wandered our separate ways until we felt a connection with a particular plant or animal. After finding our "thing" we were to spend time thinking or meditating about it, and finally we would represent this creature at the Council. To my surprise, it was the loblolly pines that reached out to me that day. I spent a long time in quiet communion with them, and I came to know that the life force is not just present in animals. It may sound obvious, but when you kill a tree you are taking a life.

Henry David Thoreau wrote many wonderful passages about trees. Perhaps the most controversial was a statement he made about a pine tree: "It is as immortal as I am, and perchance will go to as high a heaven, there to tower above me still."[1]

I love loblollies best when they're big and old. The foresters around here will tell you that a sixty-year-old pine tree is just going to die anyway, so you may as well cut it down now. That's true. It is just going to die; but so are we. Loblolly pines can live two or three hundred years, but we almost never get to see them in their mature grandeur.

IT WAS ONE of those rare spring days when everything looked perfect and new; the fruit trees were in bloom and the grass was a bright spring green. But the temperature was in the forties, a bit cool for kayaking, biking, or even just sitting outside. I decided that looking at the beautiful spring world through car windows (with the heater on) was the thing to do. So my husband, Rick, and I headed off to Elliot's Island—a place I had looked toward across the river but had never visited.

The community of Elliot's Island is at the end of a long, narrow finger of land. A single road surrounded by marshland for most of its length is the only way to get there. Along the first part of the road, before we got to the marshland, the surrounding forest was pretty much the same old scene: small trees, mostly loblolly pines, packed closely together. All the original forest had been cut; this "pine plantation" was the new forest created by the forest industry. Now and then along the roadside we saw a huge old tree from the original forest—an oak or a cherry or even a persimmon—a hint that this land could, and once did, support a mature hardwood forest. I could only imagine how beautiful it must have been. Farther along the road was a heartbreaking sight, a recently cut hardwood forest. The large-diameter, irregular stumps and huge piles of woody debris ("slash"), left to rot because they were not worth enough to haul to a mill, were clear signs that this was no pine clear-cut. Many tall, dead hardwood snags still stood as well, lonely sentinels left behind because they were worthless to the loggers.

It is heart-wrenching to see the old nest cavities made by woodpeckers in these snags. The cavities were made when the dead trees were surrounded by thriving, diverse forest. We have six types of woodpeckers left here, and all of them nest in dead trees. It's fairly easy to spot their oval entrance holes about three-quarters of the way up the trunk. It will

be a long time, if ever, before woodpeckers come back to this forest. Even sadder is the knowledge that these were the first — or last, depending on how you look at it — hardwood forests for large distances. Birds and animals displaced from these last remaining hardwood forests cannot just move to the hardwood forest next door. There isn't one.

Farther down the road we reached land so exposed to wind and salt spray, so lacking in rich soil, that the only trees that could survive were loblolly pines. The hummocks that hold these pine forests are surrounded by marsh, and the logging trucks can't get to them. Here, finally, we saw pines in the habitat where pines are supposed to grow. They are huge and stately, and their widespread branches appear like arms lifted up in praise.

It was worth the trip just to see what pine trees look like when they are not considered a commodity. They reminded me of something else Thoreau said of pines:

> Strange that so few ever come to the woods to see how the pine lives and grows and spires, lifting its evergreen arms to the light — to see its perfect success, but most are content to behold it in the shape of many broad boards brought to market, and deem *that* its true success! But the pine is no more lumber than man is, and to be made into boards and houses is no more its true and highest use than the truest use of man is to be cut down and made into manure. There is a higher law affecting our relation to pines as well as to men.[2]

Here, at last, were loblolly pines in their perfect success. I wanted to spend time with them, but it was cold and windy and I couldn't get to the trees without slogging through the mud. So I kept my distance like the loggers have kept their distance. Bless the marsh, I thought, for protecting the trees.

And pray that they never start helicopter logging in these parts.

THE SOUTHERN PINE BARK BEETLE (*Dendroctonus frontalis*) is one of the reasons why loggers are so anxious to cut down our pines. Reams of information are available about this little black beetle because it is considered a "pest." In my eyes it's just an organism that is trying to survive and reproduce. And because it reproduces in pine trees, and because we have covered this whole peninsula in pine trees, the pine bark beetle is doing quite well. In fact, it does best in areas where pine trees grow very closely spaced in monocultures. So the little female beetle doesn't have far to fly to find a pine tree.

She gnaws through the bark and creates a curvy tunnel in the wood beneath, then releases a pheromone, a chemical that attracts male beetles to the tree, giving her a choice of mates. After she has done the deed with a lucky guy beetle she deposits her eggs in small niches along the tunnel.

The larva that hatches from the egg is a yellowish c-shaped grub that also feeds on the sweet layer of wood just under the bark. When the larva has eaten all it needs it is ready for that miraculous transformation called pupation—the confined quiescent period when a soft grub becomes a hard-shelled adult insect with legs and antennae. Pupation takes place near the brown outer part of the bark, and when it is complete the shiny adult black beetle, smaller than a peppercorn, chews a perfect round hole and tries its new wings for the first time. It is rare to see the beetles emerge, but the tiny telltale holes they leave are easy to spot. The holes are a badge of victory to the beetles who have successfully completed their life cycle; but they are a sign of failure for foresters.

If they are present in large enough numbers, the beetles themselves can kill a tree just by chewing their lacy patterns through the sap-conducting tissue layer. But foresters can live with that; a dead tree is still salable timber. What really irks them is that a fungus called bluestain (*Ceratocystis minor*) usually follows the beetles. Fungus-stained wood is unmarketable—at least as timber.

In nature there is always another layer, and the closer you look the more intricate things become. The relationship between the pine bark beetles and the bluestain fungus is just another example of that. You see, as the new adult beetle chews her escape hole in the outer bark, she picks up a few minuscule hitchhikers: mites (*Tarsonemus*). If the beetles are smaller than peppercorns, imagine how tiny the mites are. But, like Russian nesting dolls, the story does not end there. The mites have hitchhikers, too: even smaller organisms—the spores of the bluestain fungus. In fact, some species of mites have special pockets in their anatomy that carry the spores. When our triumphant beetle flies to her chosen tree to gnaw and mate, she carries along with her the fungus-carrying mites.[3]

Once inside the tunnels in the sweet wood, the mites drop off the beetle and the spores drop off the mites. The spores germinate, and fungus threads begin growing on the wood, soon producing new, dark-colored spores which just so happen to be the favorite food of the mites. You see how it is. I'm sure if we look closer there is even more to the story, but I'll stop there.

So I suppose the beetles are pests. But like every organism they also have a vital life energy, a drive to live. They are not evil, they just *are*. If you see them only as pests, you have a restricted view of life. They can also be seen in wonderment.

If the acres behind your house were filled with adolescent pine trees, a forester might suggest that you should cut them down now or take the chance that they will become infested with pine beetles: "Your trees are worth a hundred thousand dollars today, but if the bluestain comes in they won't be worth anything. May as well cut them now; I have an interested buyer. What do you say? Just sign here."

What foresters usually *don't* tell you is that the beetles are less likely to damage pines living in healthy forests with a good mix of tree species and animals such as salamanders, lizards, and birds that look at the beetles not as pests or in wonderment, but as food.

WHEN WE, as individual landowners, decide to cut our forests we reassure ourselves that there is plenty of forest land elsewhere, and, although we have destroyed the habitat we have control over, the forest plants and animals will survive somewhere else. Environmental activists are fond of saying, "There is no such place as away." Likewise, "There is no such place as somewhere else." Steve Emmet Maddox, of the organization Restore America's Estuaries, sums it up succinctly: "Habitats are places where plants and animals live. Change or destroy habitat and you change or destroy the animals that lived there."[4] We need to own up to this. We are responsible for the land. There are many sad illustrations of the "not my fault" syndrome. Here I'll just discuss one—the fate of the red-cockaded woodpecker (*Picoides borealis*).

To understand what happened to the red-cockaded woodpeckers you first have to understand how trees grow and change as they get older. Unlike animals, which can grow in all directions, plants can only grow "lengthwise" and "widthwise." As trees grow widthwise, the newest cells are the ones on the outside layer, nearest the bark. These young cells, called sapwood, actively transport water and nutrients and keep the tree alive. Every year the tree makes a new layer of cells. The old cells die and the trees use them to store substances such as gums, oils, and resins. The result is that toward the center of the tree there is a darker wood with different properties, the heartwood. If you examine a freshly cut stump you can often see where the sapwood stops and the heartwood begins. If you are a woodworker you are certainly familiar with heartwood because of its density and its beauty. Older branches develop heartwood, too. Loblolly pines have to be at least sixty years old before they have branches large enough to develop heartwood.

There is a fungus (*Phellinus pini*) that grows only in the heartwood of pine. By feeding on the nutrients in the heartwood the fungus creates a condition with the romantic name "red heart," in which the heartwood becomes soft. Although red heart does somewhat weaken the structural integrity of the tree, and certainly destroys its commercial value, it attacks only the dead cells, so a pine tree with red heart can still live a very long life.

The fungus is able to gain entry to the heartwood of the tree when a large old branch with heartwood breaks off. How the fungal spores find the stub of a branch with heartwood in the center is still a mystery, but it is probable that they are carried by the wind. The spores that land on the pine heartwood germinate; the spores that land elsewhere die.

After a few years the fungus has spread to the heartwood of the trunk, where it creates a soft, spongy area. Now conditions are perfect for a red-cockaded woodpecker: an old, living pine tree with red heart. Somehow the woodpeckers can tell when a tree has the red heart fungus; perhaps it has a slightly different sound to a tapping woodpecker. The dominant male in a group of woodpeckers will make the final decision on exactly where the new nest cavity should be. Digging out a cavity can take from one to six years. When, at last, there is a cavity with a small entrance hole and a large space in the center of the tree lined with soft wood chips to hold the eggs, the bird finishes by pecking holes in the bark around the entrance hole. The holes in the bark cause the living pine tree to exude a sticky, resinous sap that deters snakes and annoying insects from entering the nest.

Woodpecker pairs mate for life. During the day the male and female take turns incubating the eggs; the male sits on the eggs throughout the night. The pair will return to the same nest year after year until the tree no longer produces sap . . . or until it has been cut down.

Researchers in Georgia positioned automatic cameras at thirty-one red-cockaded woodpecker nest cavities.[5] They collected and examined photos for five years to see what the adult birds ate and what food items they brought to their nestlings. The cameras showed that the birds were eating all kinds of beetles, including pine bark beetles, but the most common prey item, and the one they fed to their young, was cockroaches. You have to love a bird that eats cockroaches.

In the years before massive logging, red-cockaded woodpeckers were fairly common along the East Coast and inland toward the Mississippi River. But now—mostly, it is thought, because almost all of our large pines are gone—the birds are found in only 1 percent of their original range. They used to live in Maryland, but no longer. And they are no longer found in New Jersey or Tennessee or Missouri. But that's no one's fault, is it? I sometimes wonder if the birds aren't somehow having the last laugh. We cut down their trees, destroyed their habitat, put buildings where the forests used to be; and now our cities are overrun with cockroaches.

Grandfather Trees

Don't get me wrong. I do believe in cutting and using trees for wood. I am writing this on a wooden desk in a wood-frame house. I think wood is a wonderful renewable resource that we should utilize. My complaint is that our culture sees every tree as a source of wood. I think some trees should just be trees. I think some trees should be allowed to do whatever they want and should be able to die of old age right where they are standing. Whatever the fates hold in store is what we should allow for those trees—perhaps dying all at once from a lightning strike (a result of being the tallest tree in the forest), or perhaps dying one limb at a time as the fungi and insects slowly take over. We should not be afraid of dying trees. If we are, we will cut down all trees in their prime, before they get old. And that is exactly what is happening. One of my ecophilosopher friends puts it this way: we have no grandfather trees left.

Yes, grandfather trees are the closest to death, but they are also the ones with the most to teach us. They are the ones that inspire awe, and the ones we choose to pray under. They host the greatest variety of other living creatures. If you had the patience to count all the varieties of mosses, lichens, spiders, mites, aphids, snails, slugs, fungi, birds, squirrels, and other living things on one of those grandfather trees, you would find many more things than you would find on a young, healthy tree. I wouldn't want to live in a society of only children and teenagers. And most of the so-called forests in my part of the country contain nothing but juveniles.

THE U.S. DEPARTMENT OF AGRICULTURE has published a book of forest statistics for Maryland.[1] The book is filled with tables and graphs, but the table that intrigues me is the one that estimates the number of live trees in Maryland forests by size class and species class. The table shows that Maryland has approximately eight billion trees. But the astonishing thing, something I realized only when I looked more closely at the numbers, is that 95 percent of the trees are less than five inches in diameter! Five inches is smaller than the spread of your hand. To be fair, the majority of the trees are in the seedling class, and that can skew the figures, but even when you don't figure in the seedlings, when you just count trees one inch in diameter and upward, 72 percent of the trees in the state are between one and five inches in diameter. What do you consider an average-size tree? I would say at least the width of my shoulders. Only 2 percent of forest trees in Maryland are that wide or wider. And what about the big, old trees, the kind you can't wrap your arms all the way around—the grandfather trees? The sad, sad truth is that less than 0.1 percent of the forest trees

are that large. Those are the grandfather trees. They are the trees we should be protecting, but instead we keep right on cutting.

NOT SO LONG AGO the largest trees lived in the forests, and the trees in parks and yards were modest by comparison; today, in many parts of the world, the tables have turned. When I say we have no grandfather trees left, I am talking about trees living in a natural ecosystem. On a recent trip to Boston, a friend remarked that if I loved big trees I should visit their park. The park was designed by Frederick Law Olmstead, America's most famous landscape designer, and it did indeed have big, beautiful trees that were obviously lovingly cared for. They were admirable, but they lacked the magic of forest trees that grow where they grow because of luck or fate or the forces of nature. A forest tree spends its entire life, from seed to maturity, in one spot. The park trees, however, had been dug up from their natal ground and planted where a human decided they should grow. These trees are like immigrants, forced from their land, who never quite learn the language and never quite feel at home. If you are quiet enough in their presence you can almost feel the sadness springing from their loss of community, their loss of place. A park is not a forest. And a forest is not made just of trees.

What does it say about our culture that we do not let the old forest trees live? Perhaps there is a parallel between the way we treat our elderly citizens and the way we treat our elderly trees. It is uncomfortable to say, but *useless* seems to be society's adjective for both groups. Maybe we could begin to heal the wounds in our social fabric by working together to mend the ecological fabric.

I want to protect at least one forest in my community

from being cut yet again. The trees will certainly not be elders in my lifetime, but I want to know that they are on their way. I want to know that someday in my community the children will be able to walk through a forest that has some big, old trees. I want to know that the woodpeckers and the bats will have a place to live. Mostly I want to know that we humans are capable of letting some trees live until they die of old age.

"The forest is that essential fact that confronts all human beings at the end of the twentieth century, an image of the promise we have betrayed and a chance to redeem ourselves from our folly," Charles Bowden writes in *The Secret Forest*.[2] I want redemption. But that desire makes me a radical; the county administrator who wants to cut down the particular forest I am trying to save told me to "quit stirring up trouble."

The forest I want to protect is still young. Less than eighty years have passed since it was last cut. Another hundred years will have to elapse before it starts to get authentically "old." But if we cut the forest now we will have to wait one hundred *and* eighty years for an old forest. I don't want to have to start all over again.

As sad and frustrating as starting over is in the East, where we have to wait hundreds of years for an old forest, forest activists on the West Coast know that it may take a thousand years for grandfather trees to grow after one of their redwood forests is cut. Imagine *their* frustration. Is it even possible for humans to hold an intention for regrowth for a thousand years? I doubt it, even as I hope it.

I have some friends who live in California. More than a hundred years ago all of the giant old redwood trees on their ranch were cut. There are many young redwood trees left, but if my friends protect those young trees from being cut for their entire lives, and if their daughter protects the trees for her entire life, and if their daughter's daughter protects the trees for her entire life, there will still be no "old" redwood trees on the ranch. Yet someone can decide in a minute to cut old trees, and a crew can complete the job in a few weeks. Sorry, but I'm not going to quit stirring up trouble.

Oak

Have you ever made a pact with another person to look after and protect that person as long as you are alive and able? If you are married you certainly have. How about with a pet? Have you ever vowed, silently or not, that as long as you are alive and able you will make sure that animal is treated properly? Well, I have made such a pact with a plant—a tree. An oak tree, to be exact, that lives in my backyard. Perhaps eliciting human affection is a survival mechanism for oaks. The oak must be a tree not uncommonly spared the ax, considering that in America there are more oaks than any other tree species considered "famous and historic."

The Druids also protected oak trees. They believed that the trees held spirits that could whisper prophecies to them. Druid sanctuaries were connected to the very oldest oak in the forest. These "oracle oaks" were considered so sacred that anyone who cut one of them was executed. The

Druids would likely see a connection between E. E. Cummings cutting a venerable old oak and his death from a stroke hours later.

> Your last summer at your farm
> like a young man again you cut down
> an aging, great New England oak.
> Oh you are big and you would not start to stoop
> even on that absolute day.[1]

The most famous tree in Maryland, the state tree, in fact, was the Wye Oak. That white oak (*Quercus alba*) was the first tree in the history of the United States to receive formal government protection. Imagine! A tree that elicited affection from a legislative body! At 460 years of age it was the largest and oldest specimen of its kind in the nation. I passed within a few miles of the Wye Oak many times, but never made the detour to see it, reassuring myself that I would do it someday. It had been there since 1543; what was the hurry?

It is a lesson difficult for us to learn, but where there is life there is death. And two years ago the mighty oak blew over in a storm. I never got to see it, but a botanist friend pressed a branch for me that now hangs on my office wall. Its presence there is a lesson to me.

THIS MORNING, early, I saw a gray squirrel (*Sciurus carolinensis*) crawling through the branches of the oak in my backyard. When the squirrel got as far out as it could go on the smaller branches, it made a big leap to the adjacent magnolia tree (*Magnolia soulangiana*). I have witnessed that squirrel take this route many mornings. After crawling through the magnolia's outer branches the squirrel climbed down the trunk to the ground. Both the squirrel and I were looking to see where the cats were at that point, but the only animals that gave the squirrel any trouble were the birds who swooped in screeching and scolding. Cats have been the death of many young squirrels, I thought, but squirrels have been the death of many young birds, too.

The squirrels were not always in my yard. They are there now because of the oak tree. It is a cherrybark oak (*Quercus pagoda*); at least I think it is. Oaks are difficult to tell apart. There are forty-three kinds of oak in the eastern United States alone,[2] and they often hybridize, which makes identification even more complicated. I have frequently seen botanists, too time limited for a thorough identification, just give up and put a tree into one of the big categories of "white oaks" or "red oaks" without determining the species. If you want to sound like one of these "experts," all you need to know is that white oaks have rounded leaf lobes and red oaks have pointed leaf lobes.

One of the problems with identifying oaks to species is that their leaves are highly variable. If you pick twenty leaves from an oak tree, chances are that each one will look slightly different from the others. And the leaves from one tree may look very much like the leaves from another tree of a different species. Besides looking at the leaves it is necessary to look at the buds, the bark, and especially the acorns. The problem with examining acorns is that they are usually out of reach on the tree, and once they fall to the ground they are rapidly eaten—or hidden—by the many species of wildlife that depend on these nutritious morsels, like the gray squirrels in my yard.

For eleven years I watched my oak tree produce acorns and wondered why there were no squirrels to eat them. What had happened here before I came that caused the

squirrels to be absent? The only thing I could imagine was a combination of young men with shotguns and territorial dogs; both had lived here before me. Finally, in year twelve, the squirrels returned to the tree, and there they have been living and breeding ever since. I am happy to see them—the landscape is much richer with them in it—and I will happily sacrifice a few flower bulbs to keep them here.

ALTHOUGH IT MAY BE DIFFICULT for humans to distinguish oak species, the squirrels are able to tell. Acorns from different species vary in the amount of nutritious fat and bitter tannins they contain, and also in the time of year they germinate. These factors determine whether a squirrel will eat an acorn immediately or bury it to eat later in the winter or the spring.[3] If an acorn is of the type that sprouts in the fall, the squirrel will eat it right away—a germinated acorn is not as tasty as an ungerminated one. If they cannot eat the acorn right away they nip out the tiny embryo from the nut, thus killing the seed and preventing germination. Acorns high in tannins store best through the winter. The squirrels know that and hide those acorns. Some are forgotten, and they may eventually sprout. So, even though the squirrels are responsible for killing many of the seeds, they are also important seed dispersers. From the tree's point of view, it is OK to have ninety-nine of every hundred seeds eaten if the remaining one is taken to an area where it will germinate and grow.

Insect infestation is another factor that determines whether a squirrel will eat or store an acorn. A small beetle (*Curculio*) that looks like a miniature anteater feeds on acorns. The weevils crawl out of the ground during the summer months and begin climbing the nearest oak tree. They climb high into the branches hoping to find another weevil of the opposite sex. After mating, the female makes her way to a maturing acorn. At the end of her long, curved snout are jaws that can gnaw a circular tunnel in the acorn. The material she chews from the tunnel is digested as food, but that is not the reason she makes the tunnel. When the tunnel is completed the female turns around and extends her ovipositor—a telescoping egg-laying appendage—into the hole, lays an egg, and seals the hole with a bit of her poop. A small white dot, from this fecal pellet, is the only way to tell from the outside that the acorn has a weevil egg in it. In a week or two the egg hatches into a small, wormlike larva that feeds on the flesh of the acorn. Eventually the mature acorn falls to the ground. Rather than avoiding these acorns, the squirrels relish the protein-rich condiment. Some of the larva-containing acorns escape discovery and produce the next generation of weevils. The full-grown larva chews an exit hole—the original hole made for the egg being much too small to allow passage of the fat larva—and crawls out of the acorn and down into the ground. There it writhes around in the soil creating a small space where it will spend the next year. At the end of the year the larva pupates and emerges as an adult weevil, which crawls up the nearest oak tree, and the cycle begins again.

Almost as wonderful as this life cycle is the fact that someone managed to discover it. Who could possibly have had the patience to follow and record the behavior of these insects? How long did he or she wait at the base of an oak tree for the adult weevils to emerge? Describing such life cycles and relationships is more natural history than what we today consider science. How many other ecological relationships are still undiscovered because natural history is no longer given the respect it once had and our biology students are now studying genomes instead?

THE OAK TREE and the weevils also provide a food source for another organism—the acorn moth larva (*Cydia splendana*). The fertile adult female, a tiny black-and-white moth, lays her eggs on oak leaves. When the larvae hatch they crawl toward the nearest acorns, their preferred food. But neither the adult moths nor the little larvae have a way to get through the acorn's shell. They depend on the holes made by the oak weevils and larvae. No oak tree: no squirrels, no weevils, no acorn moths. And how many other organisms would we lose as well? Without this oak my yard would be a less ecologically rich and interesting place.

IN SOME YEARS oak trees produce a bumper crop of acorns—far more than in other years. Studies have shown that in these "masting" years the mice that feed on acorns are also more abundant—and since mice are a preferred food of owls and other raptors, masting oak trees mean more owls.[4] Want owls? Plant oaks. The mice that aren't eaten by hawks and owls can repay the oak for providing the food that kept them alive over the winter by feeding on the pupae of gypsy moth caterpillars during the summer. The gypsy moth caterpillars (*Lymantria dispar*) relish oak leaves and can defoliate whole forests, weakening the trees as a result. But eventually a caterpillar will stop feeding and form a pupal case in which it will metamorphose into a moth. The trees in a gypsy moth–infested forest have dark, brittle pupal cases hanging on their trunks. When mice eat these pupae, they help to prevent another generation of moths from maturing, mating, and laying eggs. Fewer acorns: fewer mice, more gypsy moth caterpillars.

Acorn production can also affect the abundance of deer. White-tailed deer are more likely to have twins the spring following a mast year.[5] Besides acorns, deer also like to eat tree seedlings. When acorns are scarce, more of the seedlings will be "browsed," resulting in less cover, and potentially greater mortality for songbirds.

BIOCHEMISTS HAVE WORKED OUT the intricate pathways of photosynthesis and aerobic respiration, and have even mapped the human genetic code; but the field we call ecology, the connections between organisms and their environment, is a huge canvas of the unknown. We put a few strokes on the canvas when we learn about connections — such as the one between the mice and the gypsy moths — but there are still far more gaps than there is knowledge to fill them.

For instance, I was the first to experimentally identify the pollinator of a particular rare wildflower.[6] I was also the first to describe the plant's mating system, the time it takes the seeds to mature, and some of the animals that feed on the seeds. Many nonscientists assume that we already know these facts about most plants, but the truth is that these details are unknown for the majority of non–crop plant species.

We are beginning to understand the connections between oak trees and other species, but we still have much to learn. When it comes to other plant species we have almost everything to learn. We have been to the moon but we still don't understand what is in our own backyards.

Maple

Helicopters, keys, whirly-gigs; whatever you call them, the seeds that rain down from maple trees are magical. As children my siblings and I would divide the two-parted seeds down the middle, then split them open and remove the tender bright green morsel within. The remaining sticky surface made a glue perfect for adhering the seed cover to our noses, turning us into miniature Pinocchios. It seems to be a lost art among today's children, who also don't know how to test for butter appreciation with a buttercup flower.

You don't have to stick the maple seeds on your nose to be entertained by them, however. Just take advantage of that one perfectly calm, warm spring day when the seeds swirl down magically one after another. Ripe seeds will fall, of course, but what makes a particular seed fall exactly now, or . . . now, or an hour from now? That is among the mysteries of nature we rarely have the time or patience to uncover. But we can be there to witness them just the same: the maple rain. A friend once stopped by my house for a visit on a maple rain day. I wasn't home, so he sat and watched the spectacle for an hour before he left. Lao-tzu would agree that his time wasn't wasted. "Teaching without words and work without doing / Are understood by very few," he wrote.[1]

Aside from being entertaining, maple trees are interesting because they are precocious—they are in a hurry to do everything. To some people the first sign of spring is blooming forsythia or daffodils, but to me it is the flush of red in the tops of the red maple (*Acer rubrum*) trees. A closer look will show that the red blush is produced by many tiny red flowers. It is not uncommon for maples to bloom while night temperatures are still below freezing. The trees are in a hurry because their plan is to be producing seed while other trees are just awakening from their winter sleep.

Most eastern trees flower in the summer and drop their seeds in fall, and the seeds germinate the following spring. But the maple does everything double-time: flowering while it is still practically winter and dropping seeds in the spring. The seeds germinate that same spring. It's a clever strategy because the seeds are not exposed to the hungry animals that eat seeds all winter long. But this early schedule does in fact benefit animals by providing energy for the tasks associated with springtime breeding. I have seen squirrels and birds eating the tiny, nectar-rich flowers; and I have seen squirrels eagerly peel apart the immature fruits to get at the tender green seeds within. Such sweet, fresh food must taste wonderful to them after the long winter—like fresh-from-the-garden spring greens taste to humans.

Most people don't associate gender with trees, but if you find a maple tree that does not produce seeds you may be

looking at a male tree. Red maple flowers don't have both male and female reproductive parts as the flowers of many plants do — they have either one or the other. On some maple trees particular branches will have only male flowers and will produce no seeds, while other branches will have only female flowers that eventually produce seeds. In other cases entire trees will have only male or female flowers. Wind and insects do the job of carrying the male pollen to the female flowers.

Red maples are also unique for another reason — something botanists call the "red maple paradox." The paradox is that red maple trees are increasing in abundance across the eastern part of North America and no one knows exactly why. Early land surveys recorded red maples as a minor component of the forest, typically less than 5 percent of the trees. In those same areas today, red maples are a dominant tree in the forest. Marc Abrams, who has studied this paradox, says that red maple is now one of the most widespread and abundant tree species in the eastern United States.[2]

The most likely cause for the red maple's population explosion is the fire suppression we have been practicing for more than a century. A fascinating controversy is currently raging over how Native Americans influenced the structure of the forests prior to their "discovery" by European explorers and settlers; there is consensus, however, that fire was a frequently used tool.[3] Because red maples are much more sensitive to fire than oaks and other species, the early lack of maples could be a reflection of the burning practiced by native people for hunting or managing the forest. The subsequent reduction in burning after the native peoples were driven out or restricted to reservations allowed red maples to prosper.

On the other hand, the red maple population increase may be related to the explosion of the white-tailed deer population. Deer will eat maple seeds and seedlings, but given the choice they prefer oak seeds and seedlings. Is the increase in red maples related to the decrease in oaks resulting from the increase in deer numbers?

We have not yet exhausted the list of possible explanations for the paradox. Red maple trees can produce chemicals that are distasteful to forest tent caterpillars and gypsy moth caterpillars, the two most serious tree defoliators in eastern North America. Oaks, which do not produce the chemicals, are at the mercy of these two species. Perhaps the oaks are being preferentially weakened as a result. And since gypsy moths are rather new on the scene—they first escaped into the forests of Massachusetts in 1869—this could explain the shift in forest composition. Is the reason for the increase in red maples due to fire suppression, deer, or caterpillars—or something else? A paradox indeed.

RED MAPLES do not live for three or four hundred years like oaks and beeches, but they can live for two hundred years. There is a little, privately owned corner of land near here that contains a grove of the biggest, oldest red maple trees I have ever seen. I think of those trees often and wonder if the owners know what a treasure they have. Someday I'm going to ride over there and tell them. I hope I'm not too late.

Black Locust

I am drunk . . . drunk with the smell of locust blossoms. The long, dull winter is finally over, the grass is finally green, and the irises and black locust trees (*Robinia pseudoacacia*) are blooming. I want to do nothing but feast my eyes on the colorful irises and breathe in the sweet smell of the locust flowers all day long. The bumblebees gathering nectar from the blossoms cannot stay away either. Of course, their efforts ensure food for the young bees that are developing in underground nests, while my lack of effort ensures that my "to-do" list will be even longer tomorrow. But still I am pinned to this place in space and time, surrounded by black locust trees dangling their white, honey-scented clusters of flowers.

BLACK LOCUST FLOWERS produce a lot of nectar. A local beekeeper keeps a couple of hives of honeybees on my farm to take advantage of this bounty. In exchange for hive space he occasionally gifts me with a quart of his honey. So I, too, get to fuel my body on the nectar from the locust blossoms. The locusts are so generous with their nectar that they even provide some outside the flowers—in little ducts near the leaves—for insects such as ants and ladybugs. Evolutionary biologists believe that these "extrafloral nectaries" must have evolved because plants with the extra ducts attracted beneficial insects that enhanced the plants' survival and allowed them to produce more offspring.[1]

Why would having resident ants be an advantage for a tree? One reason might be that they are good protectors. All plants are plagued by insects that want to eat them. But plants cannot move away from insect swarms or clean themselves like animals can. Instead the plants must depend on their own leaf chemistry and on the services of the beneficial insects they are able to attract. Ants help keep the trees clean by attacking and eating any insect eggs and larvae they find. This cleaning service reduces the number of insects eating the leaves.

A few kinds of insects, though, are safe from the ants' attacks; in fact, the ants protect them, guarding them and milking them like a herd of miniature cows. Tiny sucking insects like aphids and treehoppers get their nourishment by sticking their needlelike mouthparts into plant vessels carrying the sweet sap. They remove nitrogen and some of the sugars from the sap for their own use, but the rest of the water and sugars in the sap move through the insect's body and come out the other end as a sticky substance called honeydew, a polite name for aphid urine. If you have ever parked your car under a leafy tree on a warm summer day, you might have returned to find it sprinkled with "sap."

That "sap" is not from the tree directly but is the liquid that has passed through the bodies of sucking insects.

Ants protect the aphids for their own benefit rather than attacking them for the benefit of the tree. When an ant strokes an aphid with its antennae, the "milking" action stimulates the release of honeydew. Ants drink the honeydew, a good source of water and nutrients, directly from the surface of the insect "cows." If it is a year of few aphids, however, the ants will not starve if they are on a plant that provides nectar through extrafloral nectaries.

In large numbers aphids are harmful to trees because they remove sugars the trees have produced to meet their own energy needs. Other beneficial insects, such as ladybugs, eat aphid eggs and larvae and help to keep their numbers in check. The ladybugs will also drink from the extrafloral nectaries, which may keep the ladybugs loyal to a tree in the absence of aphids. When sucking insects do appear, the beetles are present to feed on them.

WHEN TAKING A BOAT up the river or a car up the road, I see locust trees here and there. Certainly the locust is not a dominant tree in any of the area's forests, but they always look "at home." The locust trees seem such a natural part of the landscape here that for a long time I assumed that they were native to the area; when I checked a range map, though, I learned that they were not originally found on the East Coast at all; they are native only to the Appalachian Mountains.

No one knows why the first black locust trees were planted in this area, but I like to think that they were planted as a source of fence posts. Black locust wood, once dry, is very hard and slow to rot. In the days before treated wood, rotting fence posts were a problem for farmers who were trying to contain their animals. Building a fence took a lot of effort, and the farmer wanted it to last for as long as possible, so black locust wood was a good choice.

MY FRIEND doesn't like it if you call her property a farm. She calls it an organic, biodynamic garden. She plants according to the phases of the moon, and she has an ark-load of animals that need to be kept away from the many fruits and vegetables she grows. My friend refuses to use treated wood for her fence posts because it is toxic and the toxins can leach into the ground—and from the ground into the plants, and from the plants into the animals.

How many fence posts around our neighborhoods are leaching poisons into the ground? And how many docks are leaching poisons into our waterways? The manufacturers of the treated wood products will tell you that the amount of toxin that leaches out is minuscule and unlikely to harm anything. But those of us who pay attention to such things know that we are being asked to make a thousand such compromises every day—until ultimately we have compromised away the health of the earth. And the health of our bodies is not a thing apart from the health of the earth. So in her garden my friend makes no compromises; she will place a special order for black locust posts.

Others around the world must have found the black locust useful as well. It was the first tree species introduced to Europe from North America. The gardeners of King Louis XIII of France planted the locust trees for their beauty, but now they are planted across the globe for a multitude of uses, including site restoration and wood production. Black locust trees are in the pea family, so instead of depleting soil nutrients where they grow, they actually improve the soil.

BLACK LOCUSTS are genetically diverse. This genetic diversity shows up in many ways, including the growth form of the tree (some varieties grow taller and straighter than others) and in the presence or absence of thorns. This week I looked closely at my trees to see if they were the variety with thorns or without. They did have thorns, and I was surprised when one of the "thorns" moved to the other side of the branch when it saw me looking at it. When I leaned over to look at the other side of the branch, the thorn again moved around to the side away from me. My entomologist friend calls this "playing squirrel." I found it fascinating that the little thorn-imitating insect knew when I was looking at it. We played together for a while before I left it alone. The insect was a locust treehopper (*Thelia bimaculata*), a species found only on black locust trees.

I wonder if the black locusts spreading around the globe have spread the treehoppers as well? The little hitchhikers are certainly common, but as far as I know no one has ever checked all the populations of black locust to see if they all have treehoppers. Although the idea of traveling the world to find out is tempting, the same information could be obtained easily through the Internet by asking botanists to check the trees in their area and report the data to a central location.

The female locust treehopper lays her eggs at the roots of the tree, just beneath the leaf litter. When the little nymphs hatch from the eggs, they climb up the locust trunk and find a place to insert their sap-sucking mouthparts. Ants (primarily *Formica obscuripes*) protect and milk these treehopper nymphs. By the time the nymphs mature into adults they have developed their characteristic thorn shape, which most likely evolved because it serves as a camouflage to protect them from whatever eats treehoppers.

THERE IS ANOTHER INSECT that is also dependent on black locust trees, but you are not likely to see it on the tree. The locust long-horned wood-borer (*Megacyllene robiniae*), or locust borer for short, is more commonly seen on goldenrod flowers. To complete its life cycle the locust borer needs both goldenrod (a yellow fall-blooming perennial) and locust trees. Luckily my farm has both. Check the goldenrod flowers for beetles that are slightly larger than fireflies (lightning bugs). The beetles will be black with horizontal yellow stripes, with one of the stripes looking just like the letter W. This bright pattern may have evolved to mimic stinging insects such as wasps and bees, which announce their ability to harm with striking black and yellow colors. This warning coloration may save the bees from being attacked once a predator recognizes its meaning. The mimics benefit from the deception because predators are likely to avoid them, too.

Once you have located the locust borers on a blooming goldenrod you are likely to notice that a number of them are mating. The goldenrod is a kind of singles' bar for borers looking for mates. Regardless of species, it's useful for organisms with sex on their minds to have a place where they can gather—it saves time and energy. But in addition to being a mating hotspot the goldenrod flower is also a source of food for the beetles. Their favorite meal is goldenrod pollen.

Once the pairs have mated and eaten, the females go off to lay their eggs. The female flies to a locust tree (I wonder if she uses sight or smell to find it?) and lays her eggs in little crevices in the bark. The eggs hatch in about two weeks, and the tiny larvae immediately begin chewing their way into the wood. When winter sets in they "hibernate" inside the tree, and when the warm weather returns they continue chewing their tunnels. By fall a borer larva is ready to pupate into the adult form, exit through the same hole it entered, and fly off to find a goldenrod flower and a mate.

The tunnels themselves do not do much damage to a tree, but they do create openings for fungal spores to enter. Is it chance or design that brings a spore from the fungus *Phillinus rimosus* into one of these passageways? Once again, we do not know the *why* or the *how*, but we do know that the fungus spores enter the holes made by the borers and that the fungus itself begins feeding on the wood. The wood, especially in the roots, begins to rot. The durability of the cut locust wood is no indication of the durability of a live tree. Black locusts are not long-lived trees; it is rare to find one over a hundred years old. Their life span roughly matches our own.

I have never witnessed a human dying; I have, however, witnessed a black locust dying. The tree was large and apparently healthy, perhaps fifty years old. Hurricane Gloria brought days of rain that softened the ground, and then a few hours of very strong winds. Through the window I could see that the locust tree was not recovering between gusts of wind; instead it was slowly beginning to lean. I could see the ground swell up near the base of the tree when hard gusts of wind pressed against the canopy. It was a much slower process than I had ever imagined, having seen many "tipped over" trees in the forest and having tried to re-create the event in my mind's eye. The trunk soo veerryy slowly leaned further and further over, and the ground rose higher and higher, until at last the roots ripped out of the sod and the trunk came to its horizontal rest. I instinctively released the air I had been holding in my chest. Oooa. "[E]ven trees do not die without a groan" (Thoreau again).[2]

Now that I know about locust borers I wonder if my

tree's demise was related to their activities. Perhaps they opened the door for a fungus that grew in the roots, weakened the tree, and contributed to its fall. Could a microscopic spore, assisted by a little insect, have caused the demise of a mighty tree? Did Goliath meet his David? Some ecologists, who consider the black locust to be an invasive species, have suggested planting more goldenrod to benefit the borers, thereby assisting in the spread of the fungus and hastening the demise of the locusts.

But was my tree really dead? Black locust trees can produce sprouts from their roots. I had never noticed any sprouts coming up from the roots when the tree was standing. Once the tree fell, however, some roots remained in the ground, torn away from the trunk. The roots that remained buried in the ground somehow knew that this was the time to sprout top growth. A wondrous metamorphosis occurred in the cells of the root tissue, and buds formed that began to grow upward out of the soil toward the sky. The next year, in place of one large locust tree I had about fifty little ones. These new little trees had the exact same DNA as the one that fell; they were clones. So was my tree dead or not?

I was happy to have a replacement for my fallen tree, but I certainly didn't need fifty. I chose three small sprouts that were spaced just right for a hammock grove and let them be; the rest I pruned to the ground. The roots continued to send up shoots, but I reasoned that if I kept cutting the shoots the roots would eventually run out of energy and die—saving me the trouble of digging them up.

It hasn't quite worked out that way. Sometimes Mother Nature has a different idea, and it is usually best to at least listen to what she has to say. One of the many root sprouts came up in my iris garden. I didn't want a locust tree in my flowerbed, so I cut it to the ground. A few weeks later, as I was weeding the bed, I noticed that the sprout was growing again, more vigorously than before. I tried to pull it out of the ground, but even when I used all my strength it would not budge, so I clipped it down to the ground again. It recovered, and again I cut it down. This went on for about two years until, as I was preparing to cut it once more, I had the sudden realization that this strong little sprout really wanted to live. So I would let it. It didn't matter if I wanted a tree in my iris garden or not. Mother Nature had decided in favor of it, and she knows best. Now, instead of fighting the tree I just sit back and watch it. It is amazing how fast that tree grew once I finally left it alone. Today it is about fifty feet tall and a lovely addition to the garden. In fact, it is the very tree that has me pinned in place today, the one that sweetens the air I breathe, the one that feeds the bees. The irises still bloom at its base.

I feel proud and protective of that tree—perhaps something akin to how a woman who had considered abortion might feel after her infant had grown into a strong young adult. The life is no longer in danger . . . but the recognition that it once hung by a tenuous thread makes it that much more precious. As Rilke writes:

> Namelessly, I have chosen you from afar,
> You have always been right and now your sacred idea
> is the intimacy of death. (75–77)

I have watched the saplings in my black locust grove mature, and this year they are finally strong enough to hold an adult in a hammock. It's good to have dreams, but sometimes it's good to let dreams have you, too.

Redcedar

Summer solstice: longest day of the year, first day of summer. We were going over to visit our friends on the other side of the river where there would be live music and lots of beer. That day was the quintessential beautiful day, with blue skies, puffy white clouds, and a warm breeze (I call a day like this a Colorado day, in complete unfairness to the few times that Maryland gets it right). It was a stark contrast to the day before, when the "bottom dropped out" and the sky deluged us with water. The rain meant that our friends' long driveway would be filled with muddy potholes; not that there is anything wrong with long driveways full of holes — I live down one myself. I'm telling you this because it figured into our decision about what mode of transportation to take to the party . . . and eventually into this discussion of trees.

If I were to go to my friends' house by car, I would drive

down to the end of my long, bumpy driveway, make a left onto a country road, drive five miles to where the road ends at the river, and wait for a ferry. The ferry is the oldest continuously operating free ferry in the United States. It can hold three cars, but usually there aren't three cars waiting for it. I sit in my car while the ferry chugs to my side of the river so I can drive on. The ride takes about seven minutes, and most people stay in their cars. I always make it a point, though, to get out and enjoy the river; it's a commitment I made to myself when I began working on my master's degree at a university across the river. I decided that ferry time would be sacred time—I would breathe, enjoy, meditate, see; I would never study on the ferry.

Once I reach the other side of the river it is less than a mile to my friends' long, muddy driveway. It's quite a nice trip, actually—the problem is that the ferry closes at dusk. If we should stay until after the ferry closed we would have to make a mood-sapping forty-three-mile drive through the city to get home. Taking all of that—and the beer—into consideration, we decided to arrive at the party by boat. Our boat, by the way, is just a little over ten feet long. I named her *Marshmallow* because that is both what she looks like and how she handles. In a nod to history it is also the plant I studied for my master's degree.

We had a beautiful journey downriver, and the poetry of Li Po was in my thoughts:

> Since water still flows, though we cut it with our swords
> And sorrow returns, though we drown it with wine,
> Since the world can in no way answer our craving,
> I will loosen my hair tomorrow and take to a fishing-boat.[1]

Perhaps it was on a day just like this one that he penned that verse.

The past week had been difficult, but now it was time to loosen my hair, drink some beer, play some horseshoes. At the party there were new people to meet and the usual assortment of dogs and children. Just before sunset the wind died down and the glass-smooth water reflected the silvers, pinks, and blues of the sky. I wanted to be back out on the water — it was time to head home.

Our river is always beautiful, but sometimes — frequently — it is breathtaking. This was one of those times: the brilliant colors of the sky and the water swirled together, osprey circled overhead, and the varied shapes of the beautiful trees on the shore reflected onto the liquid canvas. The sun's last light hit the eastern side of the river, illuminating a row of big, old eastern redcedar trees (*Juniperus virginiana*). First one: green; second one: green; third one: green; fourth one: *blue.* At precisely that moment it became summer for me: the female cedar trees were forming their blue berries.

Redcedar trees are among the species that have gender. They are either male or female, and only the females produce berries. So the first three trees I passed — the green ones — were males, and the fourth was a female. Her berries had actually started forming in the very early spring, after the wind blew pollen from the male trees into the tiny openings of her small cones. Once pollinated, the openings closed and the berries started to enlarge. At first they were green, then they became greenish white, then whitish blue, and then, finally, sky blue. And then it was undeniably summer.

Although I love the contrast between the green foliage and the blue berries, that palette didn't evolve for my delight; it's for the birds, as the expression goes. The blue color is a signal that the fruits are ready to eat. Why would a tree want a bird to eat its berries? Sometimes that's the best strategy for propagating the species. Elms, tulip poplars, maples, and many pines have small, windblown seeds, but the heavy redcedar berries drop straight to the ground under the parent tree. The seeds can't germinate in the dense shade under the evergreen mother tree, so birds are necessary to carry the seeds around, and they are rewarded for their labors with a bit of food. The fleshy part of the berry is digested by the bird, but the hard seeds pass through the bird's digestive system unharmed and, hopefully, land some distance from the mother tree in a spot suitable for germination.

REDCEDAR TREES can be found throughout the eastern United States. They are among the first trees to become established on abandoned fields and areas cleared for pasture. We have the birds to thank for that. No birds: no new cedar trees. In my sophomore year in college, my geography teacher noted that old cemeteries always seem to have redcedars; he wondered if there could be some old custom of planting them there. That is possible, I suppose, but the most likely scenario is that birds resting on headstones relieved themselves of the seeds in their guts. Birds, not humans, are probably responsible for those trees.

A SCIENTIST named Mark McDonnell did an experiment in which he put posts of varying heights into an old field and then determined where birds perched and "dropped" (a polite euphemism) seeds in the field.[2] He found that no seeds were dropped in the open, and none were dropped under the short half-meter posts. The birds preferred to sit on the three-meter-tall posts, and all the seeds were dropped there.

MY ELEVEN-MILE DRIVE into town—a right turn out of the driveway, the opposite direction from the ferry—is on a road that once went through corn and soybean fields. One by one the fields are being converted into housing developments. The conversion is very easy for the developers: no site preparation is needed; just add a foundation and a driveway, and almost overnight the little houses—I call them chicken pox—appear. The difficult part belongs to the homeowner trying to make a lawn and garden from a bare old cornfield. On my drives back and forth I watch the new homeowners seed lawns and water them, plant flowers and water them, plant trees and water them, weed and mow. Do they know that here in the East we can have trees for free? All we have to do is: nothing. Stop mowing. Forest is our land's natural calling, and if you leave just about any spot here alone for long enough it will become a forest, thanks to the birds and the wind. If you want to speed things along you can put in some three-meter posts for the birds to rest on. I guarantee that within five years you will have redcedars, wild cherry trees, and, if you're lucky, maybe persimmons too. You don't have to buy trees to have a wooded yard; time is all it takes.

IT IS NOT UNUSUAL to see individual cedar trees in yards or graveyards or along the river; but it is unusual to see a grove of cedars. Here on the farm I have the prettiest eastern redcedar grove I know of; it's in a seven-acre pasture that is turning back into forest. After seeing so much forest around me dying (or being converted, as the foresters say), I need the joy of knowing that in my yard, at least, the forest is winning. I have dedicated the pasture to the wild animals and the trees. They need to have a few places left just for them. Mostly I leave them alone, but on rare nights I hike out there and join the community. On a dark night it is even darker under the cedar trees; you can smell the recent presence of animals, and you can feel that you're in a landscape that humans don't dominate. It's not wilderness, exactly, but it's going in that direction. I like to think of it as swimming upstream, or, as writer Rick Bass would put it, "casting left while the world is casting right."[3]

In today's world we have carbon dioxide coming out of our tailpipes and our smokestacks—the global carbon dioxide level is rising alarmingly as a result—but here, in this spot, more carbon dioxide is being removed from the air than is going into it. Here the trees are inhaling the carbon and holding it in their cells, in their wood. It's another reason not to mow the lawn, or at least not all of the lawn.

THE LIST OF BIRDS that eat redcedar berries is impressive: cedar waxwings, bobwhites, quail, wild turkeys, downy woodpeckers, starlings, robins, yellow-rumped warblers, pheasants, and ruffed grouse. I have seen all but the last two species here. Are the trees here because of the birds? Or are the birds here because of the trees? The answer is yes to both.

Cedar trees are more than just a food source for birds. Many birds build nests in cedar trees, and the trees are also very important roosting sites, places where birds can just sit and watch the world go by or sleep or hunt. Redcedar trees make good roosts because their dense, evergreen foliage blocks the wind and keeps the birds warmer in winter. Cedar trees are important roost sites for mourning doves, ruffed grouse, and owls. Want owls? Let the birds plant cedars.

Many mammals eat redcedar berries too: rabbits, foxes, raccoons, skunks, opossums, and coyotes. Again, I have seen all but the last species here, and my neighbor claims that he saw a coyote on his farm this year. I believe him. Maryland's Eastern Shore is one of the last places in the country without coyotes, and it was just a matter of time until they showed up here too.

I haven't developed a taste for those berries myself, but then again, I'm not a gin drinker either.

Holly

You should know by now that I am obsessed with owning some property with big, old trees on it. It seems like that should be an easy enough thing to accomplish, but there are some obstacles in my way. For one thing I'm very impatient with realtors. They always have the wrong shoes on, and I haven't met one yet who is anxious to tromp through the woods with me. Then there's the fact that most of the wooded land here has been cut and cut again — and big trees are becoming increasingly difficult to find.

Last month, on the way to pick up vegetables from the csa farm I belong to, I saw a sign on the road advertising the upcoming auction of a house and all of its contents. I followed the signs down to the little village of Wetipquin. I should correct myself here; Wetipquin is more a scattering of houses and a few churches than a village, but it *is* next to the village of Tyaskin, which is a real village although it has only four commercial establishments: an antiques store, a notary, a small restaurant, and Barthine's Unique Beauty Salon. So, I followed the signs down to Wetipquin and onto a dirt driveway. The driveway went up a small rise as it cut through a nicely maturing forest! I was excited. Way back off the road, where you'd never hear a single car, there was a tiny, claustrophobia-inducing box of a ranch house next to a beautiful creek. The house and the twenty-four-acre forest it was in belonged to a nature lover who had recently died at the age of eighty-seven. The bird feeders were still in the trees, and the squirrels were scampering around looking for the handouts that had suddenly stopped.

I spent the next week daydreaming about the property, considering a purchase price, and gathering a down payment (they wanted $20,000 the day of the sale). I didn't have much experience with auctions, but everyone I knew who did advised me to have in mind an amount that I would not go above. But what amount? I finally decided that my maximum would be $185,000. After all, I would not be moving to the property—I just wanted to own and protect some trees.

The morning of the auction I arrived early wearing knee-high black rubber boots—my standard Eastern Shore hiking gear—ready to explore the area of the forest I hadn't seen yet. I wasn't expecting a virgin forest, but I did want to get a feel for how old the forest was and how it had been managed; after all, in a matter of hours this forest might belong to me. The tallest of the trees—the oaks and the maples—were impressive but not spectacular. What did impress me was the size of the understory trees, in particular the holly trees (*Ilex opaca*). Not all trees, and not all people, have the ability to grow into towering giants; some trees, like some people, are genetically programmed to stay

shorter, smaller. We call these naturally short trees under-story trees. They have to be very shade tolerant to live in the shadow of their taller peers who get all the attention and the glory. Hollies are understory trees. The presence of these old holly trees told me that either this woods was quite old compared with most of the forests here—or that it had been selectively logged. Selective logging generally leaves the understory trees because they are not commercially valuable.

Unfortunately, there is no selective logging around here anymore. We grow pines, and pines grow fastest in full sun, and to get full sun you need to clear-cut. So the woods are clear-cut, and everything goes—valuable timber, understory trees, and everything else. The dead understory trees are pushed into a pile to get them out of the way of the new baby pines. As a final insult, to prevent any of the native trees from regrowing, the whole clear-cut area is sprayed with an herbicide that kills every plant except pine. The goal of this "industrial forest management" is a forest that contains almost nothing but pine trees. This so-called management is eliminating many species of plants and animals, including understory trees. Famed ecologist E. O. Wilson claims that 90 percent of the biodiversity in a forest is lost when it is converted to pine plantation.[1]

An organization in Asheville, North Carolina, is trying to stop this "dumbing down" of our native forests. The organization is called the Dogwood Alliance because dogwood trees are another understory species destroyed when forest land is converted to pine plantation. Every day we lose many acres of our native forests, with their understory species, when the forests are converted to pine plantations. There is no end in sight to this conversion, and no one is mentioning when, if ever, these plantations will be allowed to convert back to real forests. Are we willing to give up the springtime bloom of dogwood trees in our forests for cheap paper? I hope not.

My personal reaction, and one that I encourage of everyone, is to say no to inexpensive paper made at the expense of biodiversity. We have a choice; it just costs a little more. I am an avid reader with shelves full of paper in the form called books. I am a writer who doesn't enjoy reading off a screen, so I have piles of drafts. I get a daily newspaper. In short, I use a lot of paper. I guess you could say I'm a product of my environment. Americans use more paper than anyone else in the world, and we use more of it every year.

Last week I needed paper and happened to be in one of those big-chain copy stores. I had a choice of spending $3.99 or $5.99 for five hundred sheets. The cheaper paper had 10 percent recycled content and 90 percent virgin tree content—meaning not that it was from virgin forests but that it went right from trees into paper. The trees may have come from a plantation being cut as part of its regular rotation, or they may have come from a diverse native forest in the process of conversion. I had no way of knowing. The more expensive paper was made from 100 percent post-consumer waste—meaning no new trees were cut to make it. I bought the more expensive paper. Unfortunately, I can't convince the university where I teach to do the same. The university uses twenty-two thousand reams of paper a year—enough to fill two tractor-trailer trucks—but unless the price is the same or less, the purchasing agents won't buy 100 percent recycled paper. Money is power, and we should all be using our power in the direction we want the world to go. But sometimes that's not easy.

I was in the store because I needed to print out a copy

of my book-in-progress to try to entice an agent to represent me. I'm normally very conscientious about my paper use; I recycle all my newspapers and junk mail, and I never throw away paper that is blank on one side—it goes back in the printer facing the other way—but writing about trees makes one extra aware. I didn't think my agent-to-be would be impressed by a manuscript printed on scrap paper, but perhaps she would understand if I printed on both sides of the paper? My inexpensive printer wouldn't print on two sides, so I saved the manuscript on a CD and took it to the copy store to print it on one of the machines there. The manager of the store didn't think it was possible to print on two sides from their self-service printer. Only at my insistence did she even try. As it turned out, it was possible, but my satisfaction in accomplishing my task was tempered by the disappointing awareness that I was the first person ever to express a desire to print on both sides of the paper from that machine. I know I was overracting, but at that moment I felt sorrowfully alone, brooding that no one else in this small city cared that we were turning our forests into paper, that the paper in our hands represented not just trees but beetles and birds and bats and more. Unfortunately, it's clear that we can't rely on businesses, government, or our institutions to make the changes necessary to save our forests. It's going to be up to individuals, and if we don't care—well, the death of hope is even sadder to me than the death of a forest. "My feeling sinks, as if standing on fishes" (Rilke).[2] During times like that I have to turn to the poets; the scientists have nothing helpful to say to me.

LET'S GET BACK to the subject of holly trees. We have discussed trees through the lenses of poetry, science, childhood, and corporate profits, but religion has interests in the arboreal as well. Did you know that we associate the colors red and green with Christmas because of hollies? Hollies are unique because in many areas they are the only broadleaved trees that don't lose their leaves in winter. When all the plants in the forest seem dead and lifeless and the ground is covered with snow, the hollies remain green.

This evidence of life during the darkest days of the year is why the Druids used holly branches in their winter solstice ceremonies. They would bring holly branches inside their homes in midwinter so the nature spirits could dwell with them and be protected. The Romans also used holly branches in their winter Saturnalia celebrations. When early Christian church leaders converted existing local celebrations and rituals into Christ-based celebrations—solstice or Saturnalia into Christmas—the old customs, such as holly boughs, were naturally included. But the Christians gave the holly further significance by making its thorny leaves symbolize the crown of thorns Christ wore during the crucifixion, and the red berries the drops of blood that came from his head. Many early paintings of the saints contain a representation of a holly branch—an artistic symbol of the crucifixion like the lily is an artistic symbol of the annunciation. And so, in England in the 1600s, holly boughs (*Ilex aquifolium*) were brought indoors at Christmastime and the colors red and green were associated with Christmas. The Puritans objected to the celebration of Christmas, but other, non-Puritan settlers who arrived in North America gladly used the American holly as a substitute for the English holly in their holiday decorations.

NOT ALL HOLLY TREES have berries. Like redcedar, a holly tree produces either male flowers or female flowers, and only the female flowers, if pollinated, will produce berries. The berries turn red when the seeds mature, not as a symbol of Christ's blood but as a signal to birds. And the birds do take notice: migrating flocks of small birds, such as goldfinches and cedar waxwings, rely on holly berries as fuel for their long migrations. They can quickly eat all the berries off a tree. The seeds are carried along to the birds' next stop, so we can thank the birds for the holly's wide distribution.

In an interesting twist of nature, it sometimes happens that a holly berry doesn't turn red when all the other berries on the tree do; instead it stays green. The birds overlook the green berries, which are left hanging on the tree.[3] That is just what the midge larva (*Asphondylia ilicicola*) living inside the green berry wants. The little midge just wants to be left alone until it completes its life cycle. In early spring, when the holly trees are in bloom again, the pupa scrapes its way out of the berry, and the newly emerged adult midge flies off to mate and, if female, lay eggs. The adults live only a few days, so timing is critical. The fertile female midge inserts an egg into one of the four ovules in a female holly flower. If the flowers aren't blooming during the few days the midge is ready to lay eggs it is the end of the line for that set of midge genes. This is how nature shapes her amazing intricacies: sudden-death playoffs. You lose and you're out forever, you win and you—or your offspring—get to try again another season. The tuning becomes finer and finer, and the organisms that are here now are the best ever—for this planet's twists and turbulations anyway. For now. Tomorrow all the rules might change. Life is the most complex game ever, and each one of us (and each one of the midges) represents a long line of successful players.

Layer upon layer. There is another player in the midge game. When the she-midge deposits her egg she also inoculates the berry-to-be with a fungus. The midge grows only in holly berries, and the fungus—an unidentified species—apparently grows only in holly berries with holly berry midges inside. Scientists have not been able to get the fungus to grow anywhere else, and they can't identify it until they can induce it to form reproductive structures.

There is so much left to learn about the living things here; I often wonder why we spend so much time and energy looking for life elsewhere in the universe.

Another mystery that remains in this story is what causes the berry to stay green. Is it a chemical released by the developing midge? Is it a chemical change in the plant in reaction to the midge? Or could the lack of color change be caused by the fungus—which also has a stake in ensuring that the midge gets to complete its life cycle?

Next time you're in the forest during the winter, look for green berries on the holly trees. If you find any you will know that inside is a tiny insect larva in a cocoon of white fungus that we know very little about.

ANOTHER INSECT VISITOR to holly trees—one that you are sure to see signs of—is the holly leafminer (*Phytomyza ilicicola*). The leafminers leave squiggly trails through the leaf tissue. These insects, too, are specific to American holly trees. The English holly trees have their own particular leafminers. The life cycle of the leafminer starts in early spring just as the soft new leaves are expanding. The adult leafminer looks like a miniature version of a housefly: gray and black with the big eyes and single wings characteristic of a fly. When the flies emerge in the spring the first thing they do is mate (sound familiar?), and then the females look for young holly leaves to lay eggs in. The adults live only a few days, so timing, here again, is critical. The female has a pointed ovipositor at the tip of her abdomen. Again and again she pierces a young holly leaf and lays a single egg between the upper and lower surfaces. The liquid that oozes from the pierced leaf is lapped up by both male and female flies as a source of nourishment. The females seem to prefer some trees more than others, although we do not know what is at the root of their preference.[4]

The newly deposited eggs stay where they have been placed for four days and then hatch into pale yellow larvae. The larvae begin feeding on the plant cells between the upper and lower surfaces of the leaf, always moving forward and leaving behind a telltale map of where they have been. The movement of the leafminer, like the growing of corn on a summer evening, is one of those phenomena that we understand is happening but haven't the patience, as humans, to watch. If you examine holly leaves in early summer you will see a small cleared area where the larva is feeding; if you look at the leaf again in fall you will see the telltale serpentine track. Sometimes a single leaf will have multiple miner tracks. The larvae live through the winter in the mines and in the spring complete their pupation into adult flies, emerging from between the leaf surfaces.

Now look again. There is another layer. There is an organism that can only live on the leafminer — the leafminer that can live only on the American holly tree. The organism is an endoparasitoid wasp, *Opius striatriventris*, that lives and grows inside the body of the leafminer larva. More than 80 percent of the leafminer larvae D. M. Kahn and H. V. Cornell looked at were hosts to these parasitoids.[5] The adult female *Opius* wasp somehow detects the newly hatched leafminer larva between the leaf layers and lays a single egg next to it. When her egg hatches, instead of tunneling through the leaf, it tunnels through the body of the miner larva. The miner gets mined! In the spring, instead of a leafminer adult hatching out of the leaf an *Opius* adult hatches out. This is poetry. Tell yourself again that you have a choice in how you view these little insects. You can consider them pests — or as one of my reference books categorizes them, "damaging agents" — or you can marvel at what this planet has wrought in four billion years and then at how little we understand of it.

More pine plantations: fewer hollies. No hollies: no holly berry midges, no mystery fungus, no holly leafminer, no *Opius* wasps, fewer birds, less colorful Christmases. Every link . . . every link . . .

SO I WAS STANDING in front of a beautiful old holly tree in woods that I hoped would soon be mine to protect as long as I was able. I had a beautiful morning tramping all over the woods. When I arrived at the house I found many people gathered for the auction. I registered my name and looked in my pocket once again to be sure I still had the cashier's check. My heart thumped in my chest as the bidding began. The bidding started at $125,000 but rose quickly. When it reached $180,000 I knew it was my turn and I raised my hand to bid $185,000. The bidding stalled there for a heart-stopping moment . . . and then went on without me. It was at $200,000 by the time the blood stopped rushing through my ears. A young family was bidding against a local real estate developer; he got the price to $224,000 before they dropped out.

So my woods, my holly trees, are owned by a man who made his money by building houses in corn and soybean fields. I hope he treats them well.

Bald Cypress

It was a hot, muggy July day and I was standing in the black muck of a swamp looking up at the top of a bald cypress tree (*Taxodium distichum*) four times my height. I saw green, round cones in the top of the tree—the seeds of future generations. I looked down and saw wooden bumps poking up from the muck—the characteristic knees of the bald cypress. I was thrilled—I planted this tree fourteen years ago! Standing in that hot swamp I was happier than I could ever be in the cool, luxurious stateroom of a cruise ship.

FOR DAYS AFTERWARD I could think of nothing else but time. It is, perhaps, the central enigma of human nature that we behave as if our lives were going to continue forever, in much the same form they have now, all the while knowing, but not admitting, even to ourselves, that in just a short while we will no longer exist in flesh and blood. The insanity of such behavior has only been magnified by our culture. The technological and economical forces at work in our lives cause most of us to focus on an ever-smaller wedge of time. Our global systems have turned time into what Joanna Macy describes as "an ever-shrinking box, in which we race on a treadmill at increasingly frenetic speeds."[1] We are caught in a time trap, she says, where the economy and its technologies depend on decisions made at lightning speed for short-term goals. We go faster and faster but have less time instead of more.

To understand how aberrant the human concept of time has become, you must understand how other species use time. All other species are future-motivated. Plant or animal, the most important thing for each is the success of future generations. Plants spend a huge part of their energy budget making flowers, producing nectar, provisioning seeds, and making the seeds attractive to dispersers—all for the sake of the next generation. New seedlings will not help the parent plant; some may even become competitors, eventually shortening the parent's life. The important thing, the reason for the energy expenditure, is to send one's genes into the next generation. Animals are likewise future-oriented. Animals put themselves at risk by mating—at risk from contagious diseases, at risk from predators, and, in the case of female mammals, at risk from giving birth. Yet it is the first imperative of every organism to mate, no matter how short its life span or how dangerous mating may be. All biological organisms are future-oriented because the genes that make them so are the genes that survive.

Most human societies and human economies, however, have become focused on the now. We may be putting away dollars for our children's college tuition or our own retirement, but at the same time we are leaving future generations

fewer forests, fewer coral reefs, less farmland, and less clean water. The irony is that in order to change this scenario we turn to government and politics, and to be effective in that realm we must work in the little box of contemporary now time. And that very time-style is what has divorced us from ecological time—the time we most need to be in if we are to cure the earth's ills and reconnect with other species and future generations of humans.

We learn our time-behavior as we are acculturated into our particular society. Some societies—not many—are still living in ecological time, a circular time; but the concept of linear time, now-oriented time, is spreading rapidly, and it is without doubt the time culture dominating the global business world.

Recognizing that our treatment of time is a societal construct is a first step toward practicing a different type of time. Joanna Macy, whose innovative work helps to clarify our situation, suggests that we practice experiencing what she calls Deep Time. The Deep Time exercises she has developed are designed to get us out of our now box, out of even the limitations of the human life span, and reconnect us with both the long past of our species (including its evolutionary development) and our, hopefully, long future.[2] It is her hope that by practicing Deep Time we can see our lives in their proper context, as a bridge between those who have gone before us and those who will come after. If we could all envision our lives through the lens of this more expansive concept of time, less ecological damage would be committed in the name of short-term goals.

Macy isn't the first to espouse such ideas. Many Native American societies considered seven generations into the future when making decisions. I have long thought that our political system would be improved by having a third senator from each state to represent the concerns of future generations. Our energy policy, to name just one example, would probably be wholly different if future generations were represented.

In his book *The Spell of the Sensuous* philosopher David Abram describes an exercise he developed to expand the now box. He stands in an open place.

> Then I close my eyes, and let myself begin to feel the whole bulk of my past—the whole mass of events leading up to this very moment. And I call into awareness, as well, my whole future—all those projects and possibilities that lie waiting to be realized. I imagine this past and this future as two vast balloons of time, separated from each other like the bulbs of an hourglass, yet linked together at the single moment where I stand pondering them. And then, very slowly, I allow both of these immense bulbs of time to begin leaking their substance into this minute moment between them, into the present . . . the present moment begins to grow.[3]

No doubt Macy would encourage Abrams to expand his "past bulbs" and his "future bulbs" even further, past his own lifetime, to include other species and other generations. The result would be an even more expansive present moment. Living in such a present would put us more in tune with the earth's possibilities, and its limitations.

And now we can turn this discussion back to the trees. Last week I went across the river and up the creek to visit my river-neighbor and his trees. My neighbor bought his eighty-acre farm on the creek in 1982. The farmland had been degraded by the shortsighted (short-timed?) previous owner, who had sold tons of topsoil off the farm. In many places there were only weeds, and even they didn't grow well. A scattering of huge sycamore trees grew along the lane, and a few exceptional pine and gum trees remained along the bank of the creek, where the loggers couldn't get to them, but for the most part the native forest had all been logged.

My river-neighbor has the deepest sense of time of any person I know. Instead of pouring chemical fertilizers onto the farm and growing corn and soybeans—the fastest short-term economic return on his investment, he began to collect and germinate tree seeds. Hickories, pecans, walnuts, oaks, tulip poplars, and beeches can all take years to establish a root system large enough to withstand the stress of transplanting. By the time the trees were ready to move, his little boy was big enough to help his dad. Sixteen years later my neighbor's son can already see a young forest where there was none before. He can eat nuts from trees planted with his own hands. He is young to have learned such a valuable lesson. Most people today think they don't have enough time to make a forest. Time for a pine plantation, perhaps, but not time enough for a mixed hardwood forest that will, in all likelihood, outlive them. Often, elderly people look back and see that they did, indeed, have time—it just didn't feel like they did. They couldn't stop doing what the now box required long enough to step outside it and into the future.

That's where my neighbor is different. Given a choice between two tasks—and we always have a choice—he will work at the one that will change the world the furthest into the future. His sons are lucky, and his sons' sons will probably reap the rewards as well.

ACCORDING TO archaeological explorations, this area had many more bald cypress trees in prehistoric times than it has today. The current distribution of the species is somewhat curious. The next river south, the Pocomoke River, has many beautiful stands of cypress, but my river, the Wicomico, has none. At least it had none until my neighbor came along. I'll get to that in a moment.

I WOULD LIKE everyone who reads this book to be able to relate to all the trees and the ecological relationships that I write about. But I know that my desire is impossible to fulfill, because every spot on this planet is unique. The species that grow in my forests may not grow in your forests. For a time, as an undergraduate, I thought I might like to become proficient in biogeography, the study of what grows where and why. Biogeographers are always trying to make generalizations and lump things together into "forest types" or "communities." The reality on the ground, however, is that each species follows its own ecological rules. The result is like a Venn diagram of overlapping niches more complex than any human could comprehend. Nature is unpredictable. Diversity and change are the hands she deals. The lines humans make on maps mean nothing in reality. I quickly saw through biogeography and moved on. I wanted to try to understand real relationships — what the ground really looked like.

I know that relatively few readers will be able to relate to what I write about bald cypress trees. They grow only on the flattest, wettest spots of the southeastern United States. They grow in the muck, where the water moves slowly and the mosquitoes move quickly. And, oh, they used to grow so large. Never lacking for water or sunlight in those flat swamps, their tapering, smooth-barked trunks would shoot up toward the sky. They are the redwood trees of the East — members of the same family, in fact, and the longest-lived trees we have.

Foresters once estimated that the virgin bald cypress forests the early settlers cut were thousands of years old, but recent evidence indicates that you can't trust a bald cypress tree ring to indicate annual growth, as it does in most other species.[4] In some years, due to fluctuating water levels, the cypress will make more than one ring. Only an experienced observer with a microscope can confidently age a bald cypress tree. Still, improved methods have aged bald cypress trees as four hundred to six hundred, and occasionally a thousand, years old.

I have mucked around in many beautiful cypress swamps in the Pocomoke River watershed. The trees seemed impressively large to me until I saw the stumps hidden under the vegetation: stumps from trees four or five times as large as the ones I was walking under. In 1797 an early citizen of Delaware wrote that the native cypress forests "impressed the beholder with religious solemnity."[5] I wish I could behold those forests, but they are gone now.

All of the big, old cypress trees were cut to make timbers for boats and shingles for houses.[6] The trees were in great demand because of the wonderful rot-resistant property of their wood. It was the heartwood, from the big old trees, that was most rot resistant. But bald cypress trees don't begin to form marketable heartwood until they are two hundred years old. Wood from sixty-year-old trees rots readily. Woodworkers of today, beware: the cypress wood you buy may not have the same properties as the cypress wood of the past.

Another unique property of bald cypress trees is that while they are conifers, like pines, they are not evergreen. They are among the few deciduous conifers. In the fall their featherlike branchlets, each supporting a double row of soft, green needles, turn reddish brown and drop to the ground.

The tree stands bald through the winter; hence its name. By springtime there are few traces left of the old needles, which readily dry up and blow away or decompose. The new needles are slow to appear in the springtime, but at last the day comes when little green "droplets" line the branches. These droplets are the buds of the new branchlets; they soon unwind themselves, and the tree is once again covered in soft green.

I know this pattern well because I have, growing in my yard, a young bald cypress tree. When I planted the tree it was eighteen inches tall, one from the bundle of seedlings my neighbor and I planted in his marsh. He had an idea that the wetlands bordering the creek on his property would make a fine place for a cypress swamp. The cypress trees would slow erosion and add diversity to the landscape. They would be a food source for wood ducks and other birds, just as they used to be a food source for the now-extinct Carolina parakeet. The seeds that weren't eaten could float off to populate other wetlands, he thought. So, wearing our rubber boots and carrying planting spades, we wandered into the muck and said here would be a good spot for a bald cypress tree, and here, and here, and here . . .

And now there is a cypress grove along the creek. Is it the first one in the Wicomico River watershed, or did groves, since cut and converted, exist here in previous eras? Were we doing a restoration or an introduction? Any answers—if we had them—would have to be qualified by time: How long ago? How far into the future?

Was our manipulation ecologically right? Right or not, my neighbor puts it like this: "We really did something that day." And I feel good about what we did.

Sweet Gum

As I took a solo walk through the forest, I practiced identifying the trees around me without looking up. I came upon one section of the trail that was covered with spiny "monkey balls"; that's what we called them when I was a young girl running around in bare feet trying to avoid the prickly things. If you live in the Southeast, you know what I'm talking about: the round, inch-and-a-half-wide, spiny, brown seed balls of the sweet gum tree (*Liquidambar styraciflua*). I know people who have cut down the sweet gum trees in their yard because they didn't want to be bothered by the pesky balls. Perhaps they were following advice from the Horticulture Solution Series published on the Internet by the University of Illinois, which advises gardeners that "the only way to prevent sweet gum balls from forming is a chain saw used at ground level."[1] Like most things in this world, the gum balls are a matter of attitude. If you wear shoes and think of the spiny brown balls as important recyclers of forest nutrients, you may learn to love—well, at least tolerate—them.

Sweet gum trees have many positive attributes. They are among the first trees to return after a forest is cleared. They are usually not a large component of a mature forest because they are less shade tolerant than other trees. For a long time naturalists believed that the young sweet gum trees that came up in cleared land grew from dormant seeds that had lain on the floor of the former forest. Recent studies, however, have shown that most of the young trees are not seedlings at all but instead are sprouts from roots of the trees that were cut. Up to forty young trees can sprout from a single large root.

Sweet gums grow tall and straight with a very compact pyramidal crown. Even those left to grow naturally look very well tended. The leaves have a pleasing, regular star shape. If you pay close attention to such things you will notice that the first leaves to emerge in the spring, the ones that have been packed tightly into buds all winter, are "fat stars," and the leaves that form later are "skinny stars." No one really knows why sweet gums have evolved this pattern of growth. Some botanists speculate that because the later leaves will be on the ends of the branches, and therefore most exposed to environmental conditions, they need to be more drought tolerant. A later-growing "skinny star" will have the majority of its cells closer to a main, water-supplying vein than a fat star will; and therefore, the hypothesis goes, will not be as likely to dry out in a summer drought. Scientists love to speculate, and this particular hypothesis, like many others, has never been tested.

The leaves of the sweet gum tree are food for an organism you will see only if you are very lucky. The luna moth

(*Actias luna*) comes out only at night. The largest moth in the Southeast, it is a gorgeous pale celadon green with long tails on its hindwings. Picture Tinkerbell or some other garden diva fairy fluttering around the flowers on a moonlit night, and you will be close to imagining the wonder of sighting a luna moth. Some people have suggested that the luna moth is the source of the fairy myths.

At about 10:00 p.m. on the very evening the female luna moth emerges from her cocoon, she extends her abdomen and releases a chemical that attracts male luna moths. "Urge and urge and urge / Always the procreant urge of the world," wrote Walt Whitman.[2] The beautiful pair mates for a few hours, and then, at around 1:00 a.m., the female moth flies off to lay her eggs. In the northern states females lay their eggs on the leaves of the paper birch tree (*Betula papyrifera*), but in the Southeast they usually lay them on the leaves of a hickory or a sweet gum. The female lays a few dark, oval eggs on each leaf that she visits. The adult moths live only seven to ten days, and they don't feed at all.

A few days after they are laid, the moth eggs hatch into ravenous green caterpillars that get fatter and fatter as they munch on the tree leaves. They look a bit like the caterpillars that feed on tomato plants, except that the luna moth caterpillar has a pale yellow stripe running the length of its body and lacks a "horn" on its rear end. Because the adult moth doesn't feed, it depends on the caterpillar—its previous incarnation—to store enough energy to fuel its activities as a moth.

NEXT TO THE MAPLES, with their unmatchable fluorescent oranges, sweet gums have the most beautiful fall colors. It is not unusual to find dark purple, red, yellow, and green all on the same leaf. If you have a sweet gum tree in your yard and you are considering cutting it down — those pesky seed balls — I suggest you wait until fall and reconsider.

SWEET GUM TREES don't begin to flower until they are at least twenty years old. Each tree produces two types of flowers that bloom at the same time. The flowers aren't very showy, though, and you probably won't notice them unless you look very carefully in the spring. The pollen-producing male flowers are in long, hanging bunches, and the nearby female flowers are arranged in a round head. After the female flowers are fertilized their ovaries begin to swell together and form the prickly seed ball. At first the seed ball is green, but after the seeds inside it mature, the ball turns yellow. The prickles on the seed ball then split open — resembling an open bird's beak — and the mature seeds, with their small wings, flutter out. Other, also winged, organisms eat them. The little Carolina wren, of the clear, proud "teakettle" call and flicking, upright tail, eats sweet gum seeds. As does the tiny Carolina chickadee with the black cap. The empty seed balls eventually turn brown. Some remain on the tree all winter, finally dropping to the forest floor in the spring. There they become food for the organisms that decompose the organic material on the forest floor — and, eventually, for the mother tree or some other plant.

MOST PEOPLE look around them and think that the plants on the earth have always looked pretty much like they do now. They know that the animal species have changed — we used to have dinosaurs — but many are not aware that the flora of the planet has changed as well. We are accustomed to the flowering plants, such as the trees I have been describing, as being the most abundant; but the flowering plants are the most recently evolved plants. During the era of the dinosaurs the forests looked very different; there were many more tree ferns and cycads than flowering plants. Humans and flowering plants are some of the more recent additions to the earth.

Every species on the planet has its own fascinating history: where it evolved, where it spread to from that place, and where it is located now. Some plant species are already gone, extinct; some, like the blue-flowering *Phlox* I saw in Idaho, exist only on a few acres; and others, like the black locust, have spread across the globe. Teasing apart the history of a plant species, using hints from pollen records and plant fossils, is a very time-consuming task; the histories of most have not yet been worked out.

We know that sweet gum trees used to occur over a much broader area then they inhabit today. There used to be one species of sweet gum that was circumpolar — that is, found all around the planet. Then, for reasons not completely known but probably related to climate changes, its range started shrinking. At least three populations became separated from each other, and through different agents of natural selection in the various locations, or perhaps through random genetic drift, the single species diverged into three different species with smaller ranges. Today there is a species of sweet gum that occurs in China, another that occurs in Turkey, and a third that occurs in North America. The North American species grows primarily from Connecticut south and west to Texas; in the cloud forests of central Mexico, however, there are occasional stands of the same species, remnants left from a time when the range was larger.

CARL LINNAEUS developed the system of naming plants using Latin binomials. In 1753 he named the North American sweet gum *Liquidambar styraciflua*. The melodious genus name refers to the fragrant, resinous sap produced by the tree. (The gem we call amber is fossilized tree sap.) The Aztecs used the aromatic sap of sweet gum trees as medicine, in smoking mixtures, and as incense. Researchers Amy and Townsend Peterson described the tribute Aztec leaders demanded from groups they conquered.[3] The demands ranged from gems to food products; but from conquered groups near the sweet gum forests the Aztec leaders demanded the fragrant resin. Today we no longer use the resin, nor even know how it was extracted. We have lost touch with one of the pleasures that the sweet gum tree can give.

September 11th
Memorial Forest

I live in a big white farmhouse beside a river that runs into the Chesapeake Bay on Maryland's Eastern Shore. I have been living here for twenty years. As Edward Abbey says in the opening lines of *Desert Solitaire,* "This is the most beautiful place on Earth. There are many such places."[1]

I once met a river guide who lived at the bottom of the Grand Canyon. He told me how beautiful it was where he lived, and I told him how beautiful it was where I lived. "The way I see it," he said, "is you find a beautiful spot and you stay there for as long as you can." Exactly. He didn't own his spot and I didn't own mine, but we were bonded by the power of beauty and the notion that occupation can sometimes mean more than ownership.

"My" farm was owned by a man who had never occupied it. One year he thought he might sell it to raise funds to build a new fast food restaurant, so he had a developer draw up plans. The plans split the farm into strips that ran from the road to the river. It was heartbreaking simply to look at that blueprint. I was near tears thinking the farm would end up that way, but I didn't have enough money to ensure that it would not.

The owner came out for one last visit before signing the papers. It was a beautiful afternoon, and we talked beside the pond, remarking on the abundance of muskrat dens; they were very numerous that year for some reason. The red-winged blackbirds were singing in the marsh, and there were many types of wildflowers in bloom. Don't let anyone say that I talked him out of selling the farm; it was the farm that did the talking that day. The owner, bless him, decided to find the money for his new restaurant elsewhere.

I was determined then that the farm should remain intact and, ideally, accessible to those who would be renewed by the strong spirit of nature present here. It should never become bacon-strip lots with McMansions, fences, and private docks.

Several years later, in another "be careful what you wish for" scenario, county government officials approached the owner and asked if they could buy the farm for a public park. My feelings about that were mixed. My small self mourned that if the land became a park it would never belong to me and I probably wouldn't be able to live here much longer, but my big self knew that it was right that the farm should become a park accessible to everyone for all time. The only problem was the sort of park the county was planning: *A marina? Athletic fields? Clear-cut the forest?* The park czar seemed to be totally out of touch with this piece of land. He admitted that he had never walked through the

forested part ("too wet"); and yet he was planning to cut it down. The plans he submitted called the clear-cut a "wildlife management area." He wanted the money from the timber to "develop" the park. I wanted a forest that would be left to mature.

We have many "wildlife management areas" (my new euphemism for clear-cuts) in our county, but very few mature forests. I want the humans who come after me in this part of the world to be able to experience the incomparable feeling of hiking through a mature forest. I want the plants and animals that can live only in mature forests to have a home here, too. Economists call my reasons "altruistic," and my views do not fit neatly into any of their equations. Although this particular forest seems like a scrappy young thing to me now, it will mature nicely if given time. I do not try to fool myself into thinking that the saving of this one forest will do much to counteract the ecological destruction happening everywhere around me, but it is a gesture, and we all must gesture in the direction we hope to see the world go.

AT THE PUBLIC HEARING the county council held before deciding whether or not to buy the farm, I was my big self and spoke in favor of the acquisition; but I also shared my feelings about the forest . . . it should not be logged. The deal was done, and the park czar became my landlord. I was now walking the thin line between preserving the farmland and forest for future generations (my big self) and not wanting to get kicked out of the farmhouse I loved so much (my little self). How could I save the forest without angering the czar? Legally, and without any warning, the logging machinery could show up any day. I lived in dread of that day. What would I do?

JUST AS THE FARM saved itself, so too a forest will save itself if you can only get people out into it. I offered to take some friends on hikes through the forest, and soon others shared my concerns about the county's plans for it. My journalist friend wrote a newspaper column that criticized the czar's plan. In response, the czar promised not to do anything to the park without public input. Whew. We had bought a little time and a little control. But as the years went by and the county's economic condition worsened, I was fearful that the estimated quarter million dollars the county would get for the timber would prove too great a temptation. And by then everyone had forgotten about that promise in the newspaper article so long ago.

THEN SEPTEMBER 11TH HAPPENED. As I lay on the couch unable to tear myself away from the horror on the television, my new little kitten climbed onto my chest to cuddle and purr; pain and pleasure in the same heart, at the same time. Sophy Burnham, in her book *The Path of Prayer*, describes feeling similar emotions while holding a three-week-old infant to her chest and watching the towers collapse again and again: "I hoped that just holding her, loving her, would count as prayer."[2] During the week that no American will ever forget, I identified especially with the women who had lost husbands or lovers but had babies (born or unborn) that deserved and demanded their love and joy. I grieved for us all.

IN OCTOBER, Duncan Williams came to my university to talk about Buddhist approaches to nature. He showed some photographs and told the story of a group of Thai monks who were trying to save an ancient tropical forest from logging. As you might imagine, this piqued my interest. The monks decided to ordain the trees as monks. It is a grave sin to kill a monk, and if the workers, who were all Buddhists, knew that the trees were "monks" they would never dare cut them down and kill them.

Hmmm. If loggers respect what the trees represent they will not cut them down. But what do American loggers respect? Most wouldn't care if the trees wore saffron robes and had been ordained as monks. In fact, they would probably laugh and be more likely to cut them down. The speaker went on, but my mind was elsewhere. What, in this nation of many races and religions, do our loggers universally respect? And then it came to me: the victims of the September 11th tragedy.

We could honor the victims with a memorial and at the same time save the forest. It would be the September 11th Memorial Forest. We could dedicate a tree for each victim. The trees would live for many years, representing the lives that had ended so abruptly. The forest would be a place to remember them and a place to heal, because forests are healing places. And no one would want to cut down a forest dedicated to the victims of 9/11. It felt right to me.

As I began to share my vision with others I got two common responses: one, they thought the idea was brilliant; and two, they worried that others might perceive what I was doing as "using" the victims. *Was I* using the victims? In spite of their concerns about how others might view the project, every person I talked to about it wanted to help.

From then on it was just a matter of details: where to get the names and what materials to use as markers. In these marvelous days of the Internet, getting the names was fairly easy. I had only to search for "September 11th" and a beautiful Web site came up that was created as a sort of electronic memorial wall with the names of all the victims on it. I emailed the creator of the Web site and explained my project to her. She was very supportive and most gracious and sent me the files containing the names. She only had one request: since starting the project she had become close friends with a father of one of the victims, and she requested that his be the first tree dedicated.

The list was fifty-four pages long, front and back. Merely looking at those pages brought a sense of reality to an event that had formerly been distant, unreal. Instead of a mass of unfortunate strangers, the victims became individuals with names, ages, nationalities, occupations, and place of death—World Trade Tower or flight number. These details gave my formerly amorphous grieving a much deeper and more personal nature.

I had accumulated a list of people who wanted to help with the project, so I distributed a page of names to each volunteer along with aluminum tags and instructions about how to prepare them. Simply looking at the list of names had given us all a deeper experience of the individuality of the victims, but making the tags deepened that sense of connection further. Now we were spending at least a minute in silence with each person, writing their names and ages in block letters with hard pressure on the tags. And most were so young! We could imagine the young man who had finally gotten to the top of the financial heap—how proud he was to be working in the World Trade Towers! And the hardworking custodian whose daughter also worked in the same building. And the sous chef who had finally gotten the *béarnaise* sauce just right. Of course we didn't really know these stories, but the hints were there and our active imaginations generated the rest. Because we knew that behind every name there was a story—whether or not it was the one we imagined. Tears were not uncommon during the tag making. As tag makers we now had an experience of the September 11th tragedy that was different, deeper, than if we hadn't been part of this project.

After some thought about how to attach the tags—nails seemed too violent, strips of cloth too problematic—we finally settled on red yarn. By the end of the summer all the tags were ready to be hung. I had assumed that September 11, 2002, would be observed nationally in some way, that everyone would be excused from work and school, and we would have a massive tag-tying effort on that day. But as the date drew nearer I realized that it wasn't going to be recognized in that way. I was scheduled to teach all day, and I struggled with the correctness of canceling my classes to complete the project. In the end I decided that I would teach my classes and that the tag tying would start on the first of September and continue until it was done, whenever that would be.

So on September 1, 2002, I walked into the forest with some red yarn and a bag of inscribed aluminum tags. I dedicated the first tree to Waleed Iskandar, age thirty-four, as requested; the rest of the tags I tied randomly as they were pulled from the bag. Over and over, in silence, the process was repeated: find a tree, check the canopy to be sure it is living, recognize that the tree has a life that you would like to protect, tie a piece of yarn around the tree—loose enough so the tree has room to grow—pull a tag from the bag, read the name and the age (always too young, never to get older), attach the tag to the yarn with the recognition that the dead human is now represented by a tree that will live for many years—that the death may preserve a life of a different kind. All sizes and species of trees were tagged—small ones that one hand would fit around and larger ones that took a big hug to reach around; for the very largest trees I had to walk the yarn around. On some days I had volunteers helping: friends, family, students; on other days I was alone in the forest for hours. Even when I had help we usually wandered off in separate directions; tag tying turned out to be a silent and solitary activity. But, surprisingly, it wasn't solemn. The birds were singing; there were lots of different insects and plants to enjoy; it was nice being in the forest tying tags. The forest was a place of solace, a healing place—and isn't that the purpose of a memorial forest, after all? A place where we have the opportunity to recognize that we are grieving, yes, but also to recognize that our very grief is a small but natural part of this tremendously large, complex, amazing web of life. "How even the lamenting of sorrow resolves into pure form," wrote Rilke (61). This is how nature heals us. This is why we have sacred groves. This is just one of the many reasons that humans need old forests.

WE HAD FINISHED tying the tags by the end of September. If you walk through the forest today, as I did, you will see many, many trees circled by red yarn with shiny tags hanging from them. You may walk up to one of the trees, as I did, and read it: "Marlyn Garcia 21"; and you may think about that life for a moment. It has been almost two years since we dedicated the forest. I don't think the park czar knows yet that the county has a memorial forest; he's not too connected with that forest, you see. But if he tries to cut it down, I think he will find out in a hurry.

Baby Trees

I am one of those biology teachers who show the infamous childbirth video. You may have seen it in biology class, too. It starts by discussing conception; then there is a long, boring section about the growth of the fetus; and then, finally, it cuts to a live shot of a woman in labor and the next thing you know you're looking at a human head bulging out from between a woman's legs. There is a lot of fluid and a little blood . . . and always a few of the young men in the class turn white and put their heads down on the desk. Then the baby cries, the music swells, and the video is over. But the video ignores an important part of childbirth.

"WHAT IS IT?" I ask the class. "What happens next? What have they neglected to show us about the birthing experience?" Usually no one knows; if they do know it is only because they themselves have attended a birth. It's the *placenta* of course, the *afterbirth*. And they squirm at hearing those words come out of my mouth. These are words Westerners normally don't use in polite conversation. Our cultural blindness to the placenta is so strong that a crucial part of childbirth is not even shown in an educational video. One of the reasons I show the video is so we can have this discussion. And I want to have the discussion because I, myself, was not taught about that part of childbirth. When my time came I lay there, a woman with the words *honors* and *distinction* on her bachelor of science degree, and was taken completely by surprise by the delivery of the placenta. Nothing but a little glimmer of recognition in my brain; oh, yeah, that thing.

So what happened to my daughter's placenta? I have no idea. It was never discussed; certainly no one offered it to me. There are credible reports of placentas being sold by the pound to European pharmaceutical companies, but most of them are probably incinerated along with the other hospital waste. To tell the truth I really don't care what happened to it, but in more earthbound cultures the handling of the placenta is surrounded by tradition and ritual. Why this discussion of placentas in a book about trees? I am finally coming to my point.

In many cultures trees and placentas are intimately associated. A physical examination of the placenta reveals its resemblance to a tree: there is a "trunk" (the umbilical cord) and "branches" (the branching veins and arteries). But the placenta is associated with trees in more ways than appearance. While visiting a Balinese family in Indonesia I was first introduced to their toddler and then shown where her placenta was buried under a thriving young coconut tree. "Tree grows strong, baby grows strong," was how it was explained to me. Similar customs are practiced throughout the world.

Among the indigenous people of the Pacific Northwest the father of an infant would carry the placenta to the base of a young spruce tree hoping that the baby would grow as tall and strong as the tree.[1] In Africa, the father of a child from the Karen tribe takes the placenta deep into the forest and places it on the branch of a tree. When the child is old enough he is introduced to his "life tree."[2] Burying the placenta under a fruit tree is an ancient European tradition still practiced in many places. In Maori culture the word *whenua* means both "land" and "placenta."

A fascinating consilience, but what does it all mean: Why a tree? What deep human instinct prompts us again and again, all across the globe, to equate a human life with a tree's life? Wherever the impulse comes from for equating trees with humans, or humans with trees, it goes beyond cultural rituals and traditions such as the handling of the placenta. There are many, many examples in poetry, literature, and art that merge the two organisms. Even the Bible draws the analogy between humans and trees. Both Psalms 1:3 and Jeremiah 17:8 say that the righteous man will be like a tree planted by the water.

Michael Perlman examines this topic in depth in his book *The Power of Trees*. He writes:

> The persistence of the human-tree analogy, in spite of all anatomical or physiological knowledge of how different trees are from each other, let alone human beings, points to the depth at which trees have a hold on our imaginations.[3]

The Thai monks I described in my essay on the September 11th Memorial Forest personified trees as monks, and I did a similar thing when I identified the trees in the memorial forest with the people killed by terrorists on September 11,

2001. When I first thought of the idea for the memorial forest I thought it was a unique concept. Although the memorial was fashioned after what the monks had done, they did not make the trees represent particular people, only a class of people. I realize now that the impulse is universal. When one of my fellow faculty members died, we dedicated a tree to him. When a plane crashed on the way to the Dominican Republic in October 2001, a memorial grove was planted for the victims a year later.[4] Now even the U.S. Forest Service is sponsoring a "Living Memorials" tree-planting project.[5] There are thousands of examples like this; you probably know of some yourself. I have no answer to the question of why we equate trees with humans. Perhaps it has something to do with their life span, or their upright stature, but the question is a fascinating one.

Then there is the second question: If we equate a tree's life with a human life why do we show trees so little respect? One clue to answering that question is that we don't always show respect for human lives either. Riane Eisler, in *The Chalice and the Blade*, says that dominance by an androcratic, "blade," culture is responsible for many of our inhumanities to fellow humans, both in the past and in the present.[6] I am not a man-hater trying to say that men are responsible for all our environmental problems; I know and love many gentle men, and certainly there are many women on the planet responsible for careless environmental damage. Those who are violent toward each other, however, are also those who tend to be violent toward the earth and its trees. The parallels exist here whether we are talking about cultures or individuals. If our never-ending prayer for "Peace on Earth, Goodwill toward Men" is ever answered, I have a feeling the trees will benefit too.

NOW WHAT ABOUT the young American couple with a placenta to dispose of? Sometimes it feels as though the only rituals we have in contemporary America are those we have made up ourselves. These are not rituals taught to us by our elders, they are rites we have plucked from the universal, archetypal ether. So what does a couple with no cultural placenta rituals do when trying to live thoughtfully, authentically? If the couple has planned a nonviolent homebirth and is trying to go through the entire process with awareness and intention, the latest advice from the alternative birthing community is to bury the placenta and plant a "placenta tree."

If this is what we're plucking from the universal ether, maybe there is hope for the trees after all.

Eagles and Pines

Mostly to avoid watching the war news on television, I decided to hike out and visit the loblolly pine (*Pinus taeda*) that stands near the spillway connecting the pond with the river. I was hoping to see an eagle (*Haliaeetus leucocephalus*). I have often startled eagles from that tree as I approached—distracted and forgetting to look for them there. But today I was alone and undistracted and I had my binoculars. I checked the tree from a long distance away as I approached the pond, but I didn't see any eagles in it. For years I have fantasized about climbing that pine tree and waiting silently until an eagle came to roost beside me—unaware of my presence.

I was shaken from my fantasy by the sight of a large, dark bird flying from the river toward the tree: an eagle! It landed right on the branch where I had pictured myself camouflaged and waiting. But here I was on the firm ground,

far from the tree. I lay down on the cool grass in a shady spot and settled in for a good, long watch. The eagle was facing me, and I could see that it was immature: still with the mottled feathers of a youngster on its chest and no white on its head or tail.

Watching an eagle through binoculars is a strange experience because they have such amazingly acute vision. They can see clearly for five miles! So as you are watching through the lenses you know that they can see you as clearly as you can see them. And they always seem to be looking back, as if they can sense when they are being watched. The young eagle and I watched each other for a time. I don't know what the eagle was thinking, but I started thinking about eagle nests. All the eagle nests I know of in this area are in loblolly pine trees. Here on the farm we have a few stately old loblolly pines that I think should be perfect for an eagle's nest, but year after year the trees remain empty. I silently encourage the birds when I see them. "Here," I say to them by telepathy, "this is a good spot." But so far they have ignored my suggestion. The eagles obviously like the tree by the spillway; there is abundant food nearby: fish from the pond, fish from the river, field mice, baby ducks. But when it is time to nest they fly toward the forest—and not my forest, either, the neighboring farmer's forest. They fly to the tallest tree in the forest, a loblolly pine, and those who know exactly where to look can see the tree and the massive nest built from sticks carried one by one to the top of the tree.

ONE DAY A FRIEND and I decided to hike to the base of the eagle's nest tree. There were no paths to it, so we had to keep looking up to keep the tree in sight. When we finally got to the base of the tree there was no question that we were in the right spot. The ground all around was littered with bones—leftovers the eagles had tossed overboard to keep their nest clean and tidy. I wondered whether this nest tree was the tallest one when the eagles selected it or if nutrients from the eagle excrement and debris had been fertilizing the tree, accelerating its growth.

We couldn't see inside the nest that day, looking straight up from the ground, but one afternoon I was lucky enough to peer down at it from a small airplane. I was accompanying an avian researcher who was surveying local eagle populations. It's not necessary to spend your days in a cubicle—there are some good jobs out there.

I know of another eagle's nest nearby, also in a loblolly pine tree. The tree is just barely outside our most popular county park, which is, not coincidentally, one of the few woodlands open year-round to the public. Because the eagles added sticks to their nest every year, as eagles do, the nest got so huge and heavy that during one extremely windy night the top of the tree snapped off and the entire nest—they can weigh tons—came crashing to the ground. Luckily there were no eggs or young birds in the nest at the time. I had my fingers crossed that the birds would rebuild the nest in a tree inside the park property. But humans are the only animals that understand property lines; the eagles rebuilt in another loblolly pine literally a stone's throw from the park boundary. So the nest was still on private property.

When I first saw the property it had a For Sale sign on it. The entire area was subdivided for housing lots, and one of the lots came complete with its own eagle's nest. The park manager and the park czar knew about the nest and the lot for sale—why didn't they buy it?! Eagles return year after year to the same spot, and it made sense to me that the county should extend the park just that little bit to include the nest. Good for the park and good for the birds. But they didn't. What about the developer, I thought: a local man with plenty of money in the bank, numerous properties, and many other lots in this subdivision for sale. Couldn't he donate this one small lot to the county park? He knew about the eagle's nest, but I don't know if he ever seriously considered donating the lot. I always meant to call him on the telephone and ask him outright. I should have. I told a lot of people about it, but none of them did anything, either, and the next time I visited the park a house was being built on the lot.

My mother is an artist; in one of my childhood bed-rooms she painted a mural on the wall that read, "We grow too soon old and too late smart." Do we ever.

AS I WATCHED the immature eagle roosting in my pine tree, hoping that this would be the eagle that would someday build a nest on the farm, I heard high-pitched bird squeals coming from my left. An osprey chasing a mature bald eagle came into sight, the osprey screaming her right to the area. The eagle was stunning, bright white head and tail shining in the sun. She flew toward the loblolly pine and landed as the osprey circled away. Now I was watching two eagles, parent and youngster, and they were watching me.

Things of This World

You should try my game sometime, of identifying the trees in a forest by looking down instead of up. You may be surprised to find that it's easy to identify trees that way; all the evidence you need is within reach. The forest floor is a through-the-looking-glass reflection of the trees above. Live above, dead below. The dead matter consists of old leaves, needles, flowers, seedpods, and branches shed by the trees. This debris may seem like useless waste until you comprehend the circle of life and realize that without this decaying waste there would be no living forest. The live trees shed their dead parts; these are decomposed by the many living things in the humus: fungi, bacteria, worms, insects; and the nutrients released in that process are available to the trees again. Ever notice that forest trees grow beautifully without anyone fertilizing them? They fertilize themselves with their own rain of debris. It's that phoenix again: life rising out of the ashes.

Squat down and touch the debris on the forest floor. Feel, in Thoreau's words, "the *solid* earth! the *actual* world! the *common sense*! Contact! Contact!"[1] Look at what this ground layer is composed of; it will probably be different where you are, but in this spot there are a lot of pine needles. Pick up the needles and see that they are about six inches long and in bundles of three needles each—they are from loblolly pines. Look around; you will see some pinecones scattered on the forest floor. The cones will take much longer than the needles to decompose, but they too will eventually be broken down and return their nutrients to the living trees. There will be other things on the forest floor too. What are those small tan, dry, lightweight, comma-shaped things? You may already know that they are the pollen-producing cones from the pine: the "male" cones. They shed their yellow pollen in the early spring and then drop to the ground where they, too, will decompose. In this forest, scattered in among the pine parts, are leaves that were shed in the fall by the forest's deciduous trees: maple, oak, beech, hickory, gum.

After you have touched and identified the things in the top layer, gently move that layer aside. Beneath the layer of recognizable parts is a darker, damper layer. You can still see pine needles, but they are not in bundles anymore, they are in little bits and pieces. You can recognize pieces as once part of a leaf, but the type of leaf can no longer be identified. You will probably see white strands of fungus living on the energy still contained in the bits of plant parts, and you will see little "roly-poly" bugs and worms and ants and snails; and you should know that there are many, many organisms in this layer too tiny to see with the naked eye. It is in this decomposing layer, so often overlooked, where the majority of the species in a forest live. The forest's real biodiversity lies here, but because these organisms are so small and "unsexy," they are less studied and thus are not as well understood as the larger organisms like the trees, the birds, and the mammals.

But a true naturalist will eventually try to learn about them. Rilke says in his poem from *A Book for the Hours of Prayer*:

> I live my life in growing orbits
> which move out over the things of the world.
> Perhaps I can never achieve the last,
> but that will be my attempt.
> I am circling around God, around the ancient tower,
> and I have been circling for a thousand years,
> and I still don't know if I am a falcon, or a storm,
> or a great song.[2]

Or, he might have added, a snail. Among the many forest organisms that need further study are the little land snails. There may be dozens of species of them in a single location, some smaller than a freckle and others larger than a quarter, but all with the characteristic whorled shell we associate with snails. The slugs and snails you find in gardens near houses are usually species that have been introduced from other continents; here in North America, removed from their native predators, they often become pests. But the snails you will find in the forest are native, and many of the species have very small ranges. It is quite possible that the tiny snail you are looking at today lives only in one corner of your state and nowhere else on the planet.

The soft body of a snail consists of a head connected to a large, fleshy foot. In the snail's mouth is a tongue that resembles the blade of a chain saw. With this hard, raspy tongue, or *radula*, snails eat just about anything they can find on the forest floor: fungi, soil microorganisms, insect eggs, and plants, both living and dead. Particular snail species probably have different food preferences, but we have that much information for only a few snails.

Eat and be eaten is the first law of nature. The forest snail populations are kept in check by the frogs, salamanders, turtles, small rodents, and birds that eat them. Although often overlooked, the snails are an important part of the forest food chain.

Examine a snail closely and you will see that it has two pairs of tentacles: the shorter pair, toward the front of the head, is used to explore the world by touch and smell; the larger pair is topped by the eyes. The eyes can be retracted down inside the tentacles if the snail is threatened—by something such as the light touch of a human fingertip. So the little snail goes crawling through the moist forest litter touching, smelling, looking, eating. A specialized structure at the edge of the shell opening secretes calcium carbonate, adding to the shell, increasing the size of the whorl and therefore the size of the snail. "I live my life in growing orbits . . ."

When conditions are dry, the snail pulls its head and foot into the shell and closes the opening with a flat piece of shell that has grown onto the foot for this specific purpose. Some snails have been known to stay in this "dry hibernation" for years.

I have already mentioned that many—most—plants have flowers with both male and female structures, but did you know that some animals also have both male and female parts? Snails are neither male nor female—they are both: simultaneous hermaphrodites. When conditions are right, a solitary snail can mate with any other snail it encounters. We are used to thinking of sexual organs as being at the opposite end of an organism from the head, but the snail's genital opening is located in its cheek. If snails can be said to have cheeks. When two snails mate, both give and receive sperm through this opening. Each fertilized snail will then head its separate way to find a moist spot to lay his/her eggs. The eggs are laid in clusters that look like tiny pearls. The baby snail within each egg absorbs the calcium in the outer layer of the egg and uses it to build its shell. When the baby snails hatch, the pattern of their whorls is already established; the number of whorls will never increase, just the size of each individual whorl.

NOW LOOK DEEPER. There is another layer, another organism whose genes have miraculously survived nature's unpredictable dice game. Another organism threatened by the destruction of its habitat. A small, shiny, reddish-brown fly (*Oidematops ferrugineus*) lives in the forest. It is late May, the weather at last is dependably warm, and the fly, a female, has just hatched. She will fly through the forest for a few days before she finds a mate. If she is lucky and finds a suitable mate, the pair will copulate for up to an hour. The day after they part ways she will begin to lay her eggs. She will lay ten to thirty eggs a day, depositing them singly on tufts of moss on the damp forest floor. She may live for up to three weeks, a long time as insect lives are counted, and she will continue laying eggs until she dies, leaving behind hundreds of eggs whose fate she will never know.[3]

If conditions in the forest are right, the eggs will hatch about a week after they are laid. The tiny wormlike larvae immediately begin to crawl across the forest floor. Each larva will crawl and crawl until it either dies, is eaten, or encounters a snail of the species *Stenotrema hirsutum*. Only that snail species will do, but fortunately it is one of the more common ones.

The little larva crawls into the snail's shell and positions itself between the shell and the fleshy body, with the tip of its tail end protruding so it can "breathe" through the hollow tube evolved for that purpose. Many, many things can go wrong, but if all goes right the larva will begin feeding—on the snail. For the first six days the snail doesn't seem to be affected by the little larva tearing off and consuming bits of its flesh. But during this time the larva is getting bigger and bigger and removing more flesh with each bite. After a week the dying snail will retract into its shell; a few days later, trembling, it will die.

After its host's death the now plump larva has a last large meal before casting the smelly leftovers out of the shell, which has now become the exclusive home of the fly larva. The shell offers the larva plenty of room to construct a pupal case in preparation for its transformation into a fly. The pupa will stay in the snail shell throughout the long winter. When May's warmth reaches the forest floor the fly will emerge from the pupal case and the cycle will continue. Although the fly's method of making a living may seem cruel, only a minuscule percentage of larvae are able to complete their life cycle successfully.

IF YOU USE YOUR HANDS to dig deeper through this decomposing layer of the forest floor you will appreciate how thick it is, and how toward the bottom there is no longer anything recognizable; the plant parts that make up the rich humus of this bottom layer fell from trees years ago. After digging down six inches or more you will reach the mineral soil layer. In a healthy forest this soil layer will almost always be cool and damp. That is just the way tree roots like it. A healthy forest isn't possible without the thick decomposition layer to insulate and feed the roots and seedlings (and the fungi they associate with).

WHAT BECOMES of the snail shell once the fly has emerged from its pupal case? In time, of course, it too will decompose and nourish the trees, but another use may be made of it first. A small organism that looks like a tick with miniature lobster claws has been hiding in the shell. The organism is a pseudoscorpion, and just like a lobster or a crab — its sea-going relatives — it must shed its hard protective layer in order to grow. Unlike a snail that can grow steadily larger, the pseudoscorpion must go through two molts to reach adulthood. During molting it is soft-bodied and vulnerable, and the snail's empty shell offers a refuge. At least that is the conjecture of the scientists who found the little insects inside snail shells.[4] Or perhaps the pseudoscorpions were merely seeking protection from excessive heat, cold, or desiccation.

The pseudoscorpion cannot stay in the snail shell for his entire life; he must leave the shell to eat, reproduce, and travel. When he is outside the shell he is a part of the life on the forest floor. He feeds on other forest floor organisms, mostly on insects smaller than he is, such as mites, which he grabs with his pincers. A duct in the tip of the each pincer releases venom into the unlucky prey.

There are many species of pseudoscorpions, and feeding, nesting, and mating behaviors vary between them. We know very little about the behavioral ecology of most species. The anatomy of an organism—its size, its shape, what it looks like—is almost always the first thing scientists discern; behavior patterns generally come later. The reason we know so much about anatomy is that an organism doesn't have to be alive for us to determine its structure; in fact, it is easier if the organism is dead. The live ones move around too much. That's why John James Audubon shot the birds he wanted to study. Even plants can "move" too much for the convenience of botanists, changing, as they do, with the seasons. So "specimens" are "collected" (killed) and pressed between sheets of paper for further study.

An examination of the anatomy of the specimen allows the biologist to determine if it is a new species or not. If it is a new species a Latin name will be given to the dead thing. After the description and the naming, the next easiest thing to determine about an organism is its distribution: where else on the planet it occurs. Living or dead specimens work equally well for this study. But to learn what a thing eats or how it mates or how and when it moves through the landscape, you need to study living creatures. It is hard work; and we have so much left to learn.

We do know about the mating behavior of a few species of pseudoscorpions. We know, for instance, that the males fight one another for the right to mate with females, and usually the male with the largest pincers wins. The winner deposits a packet of sperm on the ground, and either the female smells it and takes it into her body or the male maneuvers her into place over it and assists her in retrieving it.[5]

The female pseudoscorpion has appendages that can produce silk, much as a spider does. She spins a small, round silken nest, lays her eggs in it, and attaches it to her body. There seems to be no end to the ingenuity of nature. I was amazed to learn that the female pseudoscorpion actually passes a nutritive fluid directly from her body to the developing embryos in the silken sack. An insect that breast feeds!

Pseudoscorpions can live for two or three years, an extraordinary life span for an insect. They have been found on the bark of trees, living in the nests of birds and mice, under stones in the soil, and in empty snail shells, of course; I wouldn't be at all surprised if we found them in sweet gum balls.

But what if the habitat becomes unsuitable or the food runs out? If that happens, the pseudoscorpion simply boards a flight to a better place. A pseudoscorpion can be transported long distances by grabbing onto a fly or a beetle. If the pseudoscorpion is lucky, in-flight meals will be served in the form of mites that live under the wing covers of beetles. Perhaps the beetle is happy to give a ride in exchange for the elimination of some of its parasites.

The snail, the fly, the pseudoscorpion: if the trees did not drop their organic matter to the forest floor, none of them could live here. When I attempt to understand just a small sample of the life on the forest floor I can relate to the custom of Jain monks, who go barefoot and tread lightly on the earth to prevent the unnecessary killing of living creatures. Their practice may not be practical here, where the holly and the sweet gum grow, but perhaps shoes are an acceptable compromise between the tender touch of a bare foot and the crushing jaws of logging machinery.

My heart swells just to learn even a few lessons from
the forest. Earth, you want me to take you, invisibly, into
my heart? My dearest, I will

> . . . because everything here is so much, and everything
> seems to need us in this fleeting world, and
> strangely speaks to us. Us, the most fleeting. Once
> for everything, only once. Once and no more. And we, too,
> only once. Never again. But to have been here,
> this once, if only this once:
> to have been of the earth seems irrevocable. (11–17)

I am grateful to have been here.

THE NINTH ELEGY

Why, if our time on earth could be
spent as laurel, its green darker than
all others, its leaves edged with
little waves (like the smile of a wind) —: then why do we
have to be human — and, avoiding destiny,   5
long for destiny? . . .

                  Oh *not* because happiness *is,*
that rash profit taken just prior to oncoming loss,
not out of curiosity, or to give practice to the heart,
reasons which would hold for the laurel too.   10

But because being here is so much, and everything
seems to need us in this fleeting world, and
strangely speaks to us. Us, the most fleeting. Once
for everything, only once. Once and no more. And we, too,
only once. Never again. But to have been here,   15
this once, if only this once:
to have been *of the earth* seems irrevocable.

And so we push ourselves, and want to achieve it,
want to contain it all in our simple hands,
our more overcrowded gaze, our speechless heart.   20
Want to become it. — And give it, to whom? Best of all,
hold on to all of it forever . . . Ah, but into that other relation,
what can we carry over? Not the power to see, learned here
so slowly, and none of the things that happen here. Not one.

The pain, then. Above all the sadness,   25
and the long experience of love,—nothing
but the unsayable. But later,
among the stars, what good is it: *they* are *better* unsayable.
For the wanderer doesn't bring back from the mountainside
to the valley a handful of earth, unsayable to everyone, but   30
rather a word gained, a pure word, the yellow and blue
gentian. Are we perhaps *here* in order to say: house,
bridge, fountain, gate, pitcher, fruit tree, window,—
at most: column, tower . . . . but to say, you understand,
oh to say them as even the things themselves   35
never meant so inwardly to be. Isn't this the devious cunning
of our reticent earth when it urges lovers on:
that in their emotion each and every thing would delight in
          itself?
Threshold: what does it mean to two
lovers when they wear away a little their own older   40
          threshold,
they too, after the many before,
before those to come . . . . lightly.

Here is the time for the sayable, *here* its home.
Speak and acknowledge it. More than ever
things that can be experienced fall away,   45
pushed aside and superseded by unsayable acts,
acts under crusts that readily shatter
when the inner workings outgrow them and seek new
          containment.
Between the hammers
our heart endures, like the tongue   50
between the teeth, which yet
continues to praise.

Praise this world to the angel, not the unsayable one,
you won't impress him with your glorious emotions; in space,
where he feels with more feeling, you're a newcomer.   55
          Rather show him

some simple thing, something shaped through generations,
that lives as ours, near to our hand and in our sight.
Tell him of things. He'll stand more awed; as you did
beside the ropemaker in Rome or the potter on the Nile.
Show him how joyful, how innocent, how much ours, a   60
    thing can be,
how even the lamenting of sorrow resolves into pure form,
serves as a thing, or dies into a thing—, and, when it crosses
    over,
blissfully flows out of the violin.—And these things,
that live by going away, know that you praise them; fleeting,
they look to us for rescue, us, the most fleeting of all.   65
They want us to transform them completely in our invisible
    heart
into—oh infinitely—into ourselves. Whoever finally we
    will be.

Earth, isn't this what you want: to arise
in us *invisible*—Isn't your dream
one day to be invisible?—Earth! invisible!   70
What if not transformation is your urgent commission?
Earth, my dearest, I will. Oh believe me, no more
of your springtimes are needed to win me over—, *one,*
ah, a single one, is already too much for my blood.
Namelessly I have chosen you, from afar.   75
You have always been right and now your sacred idea
is the intimacy of death.

Look, I'm alive. On what? Neither childhood nor future
becomes less. . . . . Overabundant being
wells up in my heart.   80

RAINER MARIA RILKE

TRANSLATED BY GALWAY KINNELL AND HANNAH LIEBMAN

Old-Growth Air

1. E. E. Cummings, "i thank you God for this most amazing day," in *100 Selected Poems by E. E. Cummings* (New York: Grove Press, 1959), 82.

2. Y. Ohtsuka, Noriyuki Yabunaka, and Shigeru Takayama, "Shinrin-yoku (Forest-Air Bathing and Walking) Effectively Decreases Blood Glucose Levels in Diabetic Patients," *International Journal of Biometeorology* 41, no. 3 (1998): 125–27.

3. D. Helmig and J. Arey, "Organic Chemicals in the Air at Whitaker's Forest — Sierra Nevada Mountains California," *Science of the Total Environment* 112, nos. 2–3 (1992): 233–50.

4. Michael Pollan, *The Botany of Desire* (New York: Random House, 2001).

5. Rainer Maria Rilke, "The Ninth Elegy," in *The Essential Rilke*, sel. and trans. Galway Kinnell and Hannah Liebmann (Hopewell: Ecco Press, 1999), 131–35; printed in its entirety in the appendix of this book. Hereafter, I refer to quotations from it by line numbers.

Tulip Poplar

1. Julia Butterfly Hill, *The Legacy of Luna: The Story of a Tree, a Woman, and the Struggle to Save the Redwoods* (San Francisco: Harper, 2000).

2. Charles Bowden, *The Secret Forest* (Albuquerque: University of New Mexico Press, 1993), 54.

3. Ibid., 119–20.

Tree Hugger

1. Parker Palmer, *The Courage to Teach: Exploring the Inner Landscape of a Teacher's Life* (San Francisco: Jossey-Bass, 1998), 2.

Sycamore

1. Joy Gilchrist, "The Pringle Brothers and the Sycamore Tree," in www.hackerscreek.com/pringle.htm, accessed May 3, 2003.

2. Allen Kurta, Joseph Kath, Eric L. Smith, Rodney Foster, Michael W. Orick, and Ronald Ross, "A Maternity Roost of the Endangered Indiana Bat (*Myotis sodalis*) in an Unshaded, Hollow, Sycamore Tree (*Platanus occidentalis*)," *American Midland Naturalist* 130 (1993): 405–7.

3. Mark S. McClure, "Biology of *Erythroneura lawsoni* (Homoptera: Cicadellidae) and Coexistence in the Sycamore Leaf-Feeding Guild," *Environmental Entomology* 3, no. 1 (1974): 59–68.

4. W. G. Wellington, "Conditions Governing the Distribution of Insects in the Free Atmosphere," *Canadian Entomologist* 77 (1945): 7–15.

5. R. A. J. Taylor and D. Reling, "Preferred Wind Direction of Long Distance Leafhopper (*Empoasca fabae*) Migrants and Its Relevance to the Return Migration of Small Insects," *Journal of Animal Ecology* 55 (1986): 1103–14.

Beech

1. Anne M. Maglia, "Ontogeny and Feeding Ecology of the Red-backed Salamander, *Plethodon cinereus*," *Copeia* 1996, no. 3 (1996): 576–86.

2. James H. Harding and J. Alan Holman, *Michigan Frogs, Toads, and Salamanders: A Field Guide and Pocket Reference* (East Lansing: Michigan State University, 1992).

3. John Travis, "Salamander Moms Use Bacteria to Save Eggs from Fungi," *Science News* 163 (2003): 366.

4. James D. Ackerman and Michael R. Mesler, "Pollination

Biology of *Listera cordata* (Orchidaceae)," *American Journal of Botany* 66, no. 7 (1979): 820–24.

5. Janisse Ray, *Ecology of a Cracker Childhood* (Minneapolis: Milkweed Editions, 1999), 123.

6. C. Maser and Z. Maser, "Interactions among Squirrels, Mycorrhizal Fungi, and Coniferous Forests in Oregon," *Great Basin Naturalist* 48 (1988): 358–69.

7. Rainer Maria Rilke, "What Survives," in *The Migration of Powers,* trans. A. Poulin Jr. (Port Townsend, Wash.: Graywolf Press, 1984), 43.

Pine

1. Henry David Thoreau, *The Maine Woods,* ed. Joseph Moldenhauer (Princeton: Princeton University Press, 1974), 122.

2. Ibid., 121.

3. John C. Moser and J. Robert Bridges, "*Tarsonemus* (Acarina: Tarsonemidae) Mites Phoretic on the Southern Pine Beetle (Coleoptera: Scolytidae): Attachment Sites and Numbers of Bluestain (Ascomycetes: Ophiostomataceae) Ascospores Carried," *Proceedings of the Entomological Society of Washington* 88, no. 2 (1986): 297–99.

4. Maryland Coastal Bays Program, "Habitat Workshop Sets Restoration Goals," *Solutions* (Spring 2003): 3.

5. Jim Hanula, *Southern Research Station Highlights from the Red-Cockaded Woodpecker Symposium* (2003), www.srs.fs.usda.gov, accessed April 8, 2003.

Grandfather Trees

1. Thomas S. Frieswyk, *Forest Statistics for Maryland: 1986 and 1999* (Resource Bulletin NE-154; Newtown Square, Pa.: U.S. Department of Agriculture, Forest Service, Northeastern Research Station, 2001).

2. Charles Bowden, *The Secret Forest* (Albuquerque: University of New Mexico Press, 1993), 51.

Oak

1. John Logan, "Poem, Slow to Come, on the Death of Cummings (1894–1962)," in *Only the Dreamer Can Change the Dream* (New York: Ecco Press, 1981), 139.

2. Howard Miller and Samuel Lamb, *Oaks of North America* (Happy Camp, Calif.: Naturegraph Publishers, 1985), 47.

3. Michael Steele and Peter Smallwood, "What Are Squirrels Hiding?" *Natural History* 10 (1994): 40–44.

4. Richard S. Ostfeld, Clive G. Jones, and Jerry O. Wolff, "Of Mice and Mast," *BioScience* 46, no. 5 (1996): 323–30.

5. Ibid., 325.

6. Joan E. Maloof, "The Reproductive Biology of a North American Subalpine Plant: *Corydalis caseana* A. Gray subsp. *brandegei* (S. Watson) G. B. Ownbey," *Plant Species Biology* 15, no. 3 (2000): 281–88.

Maple

1. Lao Tsu, *Tao Te Ching*, trans. Gia-Fu Feng and Jane English (New York: Random House, 1997), 82.

2. Marc D. Abrams, "The Red Maple Paradox," *BioScience* 48, no. 5 (1998): 1–18.

3. Matt Rasmussen, "The Long Reach of Humanity," *Forest Magazine* (March/April 2000): 14–19.

Black Locust

1. Robert W. Pemberton and Natalia Vandenberg, "Extrafloral Nectar Feeding by Ladybird Beetles (Coleoptera: Coccinellidae)," *Proceedings of the Entomological Society of Washington* 95, no. 2 (1993): 139–51.

2. Henry David Thoreau, "Thoreau Journal: December 30, 1851 [The Death of a Tree]." Excerpt from *The Writings of Henry David Thoureau*, ed. Bradford Torrey, vol. 3, September 16, 1851–April 30, 1852 (1906), 163.

Redcedar

1. Li Po, "Farewell to Secretary Shu-yun at the Hsieh Tiao Villa in Hsuan-Chou" (lines 9–12 of 12), in *Of All Things Most Yielding*, ed. David Brower (New York: Friends of the Earth, 1975), 117.

2. Mark McDonnell, "Old Field Vegetation Height and the Dispersal Pattern of Bird-Disseminated Woody Plants," *Bulletin of the Torrey Botanical Club* 113, no. 1 (1986): 6–11.

3. Rick Bass, *Brown Dog of the Yaak* (Minneapolis: Milkweed Editions, 1999).

Holly

1. Quoted by Andrew George, editorial, *Asheville-Citizen Times*, April 9, 2002; also available at http://www.dogwoodalliance.org/editorial_1.asp.

2. Rainer Maria Rilke, "Moving Forward," in *Selected Poems of Rainer Maria Rilke*, trans. Robert Bly (New York: Harper and Row, 1981), 101.

3. Vera Krischik, Eric McCloud, and John Davidson, "Selective Avoidance by Vertebrate Frugivores of Green Holly Berries Infested with a Cecidomyiid Fly (Diptera: Cecidomyiidae)," *American Midland Naturalist* 121 (1989): 350–54.

4. G. Valladares and J. H. Lawton, "Host-plant Selection in the Holly Leafminer: Does Mother Know Best?" *Journal of Animal Ecology* 60, no. 1 (1991): 227–40.

5. D. M. Kahn and H. V. Cornell, "Leafminers: Early Leaf Abscission, and Parasitoids: A Tritrophic Interaction," *Ecology* 70, no. 5 (1989): 1219–26.

Bald Cypress

1. Joanna Macy, *World as Lover, World as Self* (Berkeley: Parallax Press, 1991), 206.

2. Ibid., 226–37; Joanna Macy and Molly Young Brown, *Coming Back to Life: Practices to Reconnect Our Lives, Our World* (Gabrioloa Island, Canada: New Society Publishers, 1998), 135–48.

3. David Abram, *The Spell of the Sensuous* (New York: Vintage Books, 1996), 202–3.

4. Grace Brush, Cecilia Lenk, and Joanne Smith, "The Natural Forests of Maryland: An Explanation of the Vegetation Map of Maryland," *Ecological Monographs* 50, no. 1 (1980): 77–92.

5. Jane Scott, *Between Ocean and Bay: A Natural History of Delmarva* (Centreville, Md.: Tidewater Press, 1991), 138.

6. Ibid., 32.

Sweet Gum

1. From www.solutions.uiuc.edu, "Yard and Garden: Sweet Gum Balls — Removing," accessed June 28, 2004.

2. Walt Whitman, "Song of Myself," in *Leaves of Grass* (New York: Doubleday, Doran, 1940), 36.

3. Amy A. Peterson and A. Townsend Peterson, "Aztec Exploitation of Cloud Forests: Tributes of Liquidambar Resin and Quetzal Feathers," *Global Ecology and Biogeography Letters* 2 (1992): 165–73.

September 11th Memorial Forest

1. Edward Abbey, *Desert Solitaire* (Layton, Utah: Peregrine Smith, 1981), 1.

2. Sophy Burnham, *The Path of Prayer* (New York: Viking Compass, 2002), 166.

Baby Trees

1. Brian Doyle, "How It Is," *Orion* (May/June 2003): 80.

2. Cormac Cullian, *Wild Law* (South Africa: Siber Ink, 2002).

3. Michael Perlman, *The Power of Trees: The Reforesting of the Soul* (Dallas: Spring Publications, 1994), 38.

4. Verena Dobnik, "1 Year Later, Flight 587 Victims Remembered," *Salisbury (Md.) Daily Times,* October 10, 2002.

5. www.livingmemorialsproject.net, accessed September 3, 2004.

6. Riane Eisler, *The Chalice and the Blade* (New York: HarperCollins, 1988).

Things of This World

1. Henry David Thoreau, *The Maine Woods,* ed. Joseph Moldenhauer (Princeton: Princeton University Press, 1974), 70.

2. Rainer Maria Rilke, "(I Live my Life in Growing Orbits)," in *Selected Poems of Rainer Maria Rilke,* trans. Robert Bly (New York: Harper and Row, 1981), 13.

3. B. A. Foote, "Biology of *Oidematops ferrugineus* (Diptera: Sciomyzidae), a Parasitoid Enemy of the Land Snail *Stenotrema hirsutum* (Mollusca: Polygyridae)," *Proceedings of the Entomological Society of Washington* 79, no. 4 (1977): 609–19.

4. Ralph W. Taylor, Michael Sweeney, and Clement L. Counts III, "Use of Empty Gastropod Shells (Polygridae) by Pseudoscorpions," *Nautilus* 91, no. 3 (1977): 115.

5. R. L. Smith, *Venomous Animals of Arizona* (Tucson: University of Arizona Press, 1982).

ACKNOWLEDGMENTS

My thanks to all of the scientists who did the years of patient, difficult work necessary to uncover these stories and share them.

Thanks also to the many, many writers who have inspired my life and work. A few of them I know in person, but most I know only through their work. I cannot list them all, but I would especially like to acknowledge Rick Bass, Annie Dillard, Tom Horton, Barbara Kingsolver, Paul Krafel, Gary Paul Nabhan, Richard Nelson, Carl Safina, and Terry Tempest Williams.

I thank my colleagues and the librarians and administrators at Salisbury University for their support and enthusiasm. Special thanks to James Hatley and Michael Waters for showing me what a writing life looks like.

I thank all of the kind editors who have accepted, and improved, my work. Maureen McNeil read and edited a very early version of this manuscript. A very special thank-you to David Rothenberg of Terra Nova Press, who believed in my writing at a very pivotal point, and to Christa Frangiamore, University of Georgia Press, who is something akin to the guardian angel of this book.

I thank the Maryland Department of Natural Resources for paying me to be in the forest for many hours. I would also like to acknowledge all of the wonderful botanists whom I have had the pleasure of spending time with in the field, particularly Matthew Cimino, Wesley Knapp, Wayne Phillips, Doug Samson, Bill Sipple, Dick Weigand, and Ron Wilson.

I thank my dear friends, many of whom are mentioned in these pages. Again, space does not allow me to list them all, but I must mention Kaye and Lloyd Byrd, Holiday and Christopher Johnson, David McDaniel, and Vanessa and Wesley White.

My large family has been completely supportive and I thank you all: parents, children, siblings, in-laws. I am so blessed to be in your midst.

But, of course, my deepest thanks are saved for Rick Maloof, the love of my life.

Previously published essays from this collection have been revised from the original versions:

"Old Growth Air." *Terrain.org: A Journal of Natural and Built Environments* 14 (Winter/Spring 2004).

"The September 11th Memorial Forest." *Ecopoetics* 3 (Winter 2003): 116–22.

"Things of the World: Snails and Sweetgum." *Interdisciplinary Studies in Literature and Environment* 12, no. 1 (Winter 2005): 167–76.